American Football Language

American Football Language

The Jargon Explained

Bill Shefski

Stanley Paul
London Melbourne Auckland Johannesburg

Stanley Paul & Co. Ltd

An imprint of Century Hutchinson Ltd

Brookmount House, 62–65 Chandos Place,
Covent Garden, London WC2N 4NW

Century Hutchinson Australia (Pty) Ltd
PO Box 496, 16–22 Church Street, Hawthorn,
Melbourne, Victoria 3122

Century Hutchinson New Zealand Ltd
32–34 View Road, PO Box 40–086,
Glenfield, Auckland 10

Century Hutchinson South Africa (Pty) Ltd
PO Box 337, Bergvlei 2012, South Africa

First published in the USA in 1978 by
Running Press Book Publishers
125 South 22nd Street
Philadelphia, PA 19103
Copyright © 1978, 1987 by Running Press
First published in UK by Stanley Paul, 1987

Set in Century Textbook
Printed and bound in USA by Port City Press,
Baltimore, Maryland, USA

British Library Cataloguing in Publication Data
Shefski, Bill
    American football language: the jargon explained.
    1 Football—Dictionaries
    I Title
796.332,21 GV 951

ISBN 0 09 172617 4

Preface

"The *quarterback read Will walking away, checked off,* and *audibled* to a *counter play.* The *ball carrier slanted* for the *yardage* needed for a *first down.*"

Even a simple play can confuse the novice football fan. Yet a sentence similar to the above sample is apt to be heard on any telecast or read in any Monday morning story detailing your favorite team's most recent performance.

The italicized words and phrases are bits and pieces of the sporting world's most complicated vocabulary. Football, be it sandlot or professional, has a language all its own. The simple fact that The Game can take a noun out of Webster's Dictionary and use it as a verb speaks for its individuality. *Audible* has become a verb in the conversation of those who play, coach, write, and speak The Game.

Talking football, not playing football, is our national pastime in the autumn and early winter. It is fascinating that so many people can find so many things to say about a mere two hours of action during the week-long lull between games.

I have avoided listing the highly technical terms used by players and coaches. This work has been confined to terms, jargon, and slang that the ordinary fan may chance upon in his or her living room while watching TV or on the subway while reading the morning paper. The amateur and professional games generally use similar language. I have specified all instances in which terms differ because of differences in play.

In order to make descriptions of many of the physical terms more explicit, I have included basic coaching and philosophy. A lifetime of football involvement has been culled to produce this glossary, which can turn a novice fan into a knowledgeable fan in one reading.

—*Bill Shefski*

About the Author

Bill Shefski has been a professional sports writer for twenty-five years. He has freelanced for Pro Quarterback *magazine and* Pro Football Digest, *and from 1960 through 1973 he covered pro football for the* Philadelphia Daily News.

NOTE: *Italics* are used to indicate that a term in a definition is defined elsewhere in the glossary.

A lot of offense. Descriptive of a game in which neither team can prevent the offensive movement of the opponent.

Accelerate. To increase speed; to exhibit a surprising burst of speed.

Accuracy. The degree of efficiency generally used to measure the work of a passer, a punter, or an official.

Advance. To move the ball forward; to gain yardage.

Aerial. Refers to *forward pass* in the language of writers and announcers.

Aerial circus. A phrase used by the media to describe a game in which the ball is thrown more than it is rushed.

Aerial game. A phrase used to cover a team's forward passing attack in its entirety.

AFC. American Football Conference. See under *National Football League*.

A-formation. An outmoded offensive backfield pattern similar to the *shotgun* alignment, in which the backs line up in the form of an A. The tailback or deep receiving back is set six yards behind the center, and a back lines up behind each tackle. The remaining back sets behind either guard, two yards deep. This set-up is known in amateur football as the short punt formation.

Against the grain. The strategic act of a ball carrier who suddenly changes course, defying defensive pursuit by darting directly into it. The shock value often causes tacklers to over-run the ball carrier.

Agent. The representative of a player or a coach who handles financial dealings such as contract talks with the front office of a professional organization. In exchange for the service, the representative often takes a percentage of a client's earnings for the duration of a defined period.

Aggressive. Possessing a degree of initiative; said of an individual player or team playing either offense or defense.

Agility. The inbred quickness of a bulky player that enables him to move into position to defeat another player's tackle. This term is generally used to describe linemen and linebackers.

All-purpose shoe. Athletic footwear designed to be worn by players on both natural and artificial surfaces. The top is made of soft animal skin. The bottom is molded plastic with modified protrusions that permit adequate penetration in natural surface for fair traction yet do not prevent use on an impenetrable artificial surface.

All-star. A player who is established as the best at his position in a ballot of his peers or in a poll of coaches or knowledgeable representatives of the news media.

American Football Conference (AFC). One of the two major subdivisions of the *National Football League*.

Amortization. Tax relief granted by the Internal Revenue Service in 1954 to people who purchase a professional franchise. The benefit allows the owner to declare as a liability the natural deterioration of his athletes' physical and contractual worth over a seven-year period.

Analyst. A commentator on a television or radio broadcast who supplements the play-by-play report with a detailed review of the game's important events.

Anchor. Nickname for the offensive center, who is considered the mainstay (anchor) of the offensive line.

Angle blocking. An offensive player's adroit positioning of his body, which gives him a side angle and cutoff position. He uses angle blocking to prevent a defensive player from reaching the point of advancement of the ball. A crossing action between two blockers often enhances the execution of the maneuver.

Angling for the corner. Punting strategy designed to place the opponent in a precarious position deep in his own territory. The punter sacrifices distance for precision by trying to make the ball roll dead in the area bounded by either sideline and the goal line or he tries to make it roll out of bounds.

Angling for the sideline. An obtuse route taken by a pass receiver or ball carrier in an effort to escape the majority of defensive players positioned in the center of the field. Defensive players use a similar slanted route whenever they are trying to stop a breakaway offensive player from scoring along the sideline.

Animal. Slang for a player whose ferocious hunger for physical contact is exceeded only by his natural ability to block and tackle.

Area blocking. The assignment of blocking responsibility according to field area rather than to the opponent's defensive position. The procedure is used mostly in specialty team functions such as kickoff returns, punt returns, placement protection, and pass protection.

Arm tackle. The cardinal sin of defensive tackling, which is committed when a player reaches out to stop a rusher with his arms and hands rather than using his head and shoulders to make impact. It normally can be interpreted as a sign of fear on the part of the sinner.

Arrow. A short pass route run by the tight end, who shoots toward the sideline at a narrow angle, exploiting the upfield route of the flanker, who in turn shields the tight end temporarily from defensive coverage.

Assassin. A defensive player who has earned a reputation for using malicious tactics such as illegal forearm shivers, noseguard pulling, and illegal clipping.

Assignment. A player's responsibilty on an offensive or defensive play.

Assistant coach. A member of the coaching staff who supervises a designated part of a team's game. His responsibilities include teaching fundamentals to the players and helping the head coach to piece together a game plan, in addition to handling a specific area of the bench procedure during a game.

Astroturf. An artificial surface composed of synthetic grass, which repels moisture and is playable in all weather. Astroturf, one of the earliest and most popular of synthetic grasses, receives its name from the Astrodome in Houston.

Athletic director (A.D.). The head of the athletic department at a high school or university. His duties include hiring and firing coaches, scheduling contests in all sports and making and controlling policy and athletic scholarship allotments.

Attack. The offensive movement of a team.

Audible. A vocal change of signals made at the line of scrimmage by the quarterback when he determines that the defensive alignment may be exploited more thoroughly by a play other than the one selected in the huddle. The oral signal usually is a coded message consisting of a mixture of colors and numbers. The noun "audible" has been transformed into an action verb in football jargon: "He audibled at the line of scrimmage."

Automatic. A pre-arranged change of signals at the line of scrimmage, dictated by the opponent's offensive or defensive alignment. In many cases, an *audible* is unnecessary because the play best suited for exploitation of the alignment normally involves only a few players. For example, if a wide gap is spotted in the center of the defensive line, the quarterback and center automatically exploit the weakness by performing a *quarterback sneak*.

Automatic touchback. Occurs whenever a kickoff or a punt goes beyond the receiving team's end zone, or when the ball is ruled legally dead in the receiving team's end zone, in which case it is put into play on the receiving team's 20-yard line.

Back (B). A member of either the offensive or defensive backfield. Generally, they are the fastest, most agile players on the team. On offense, they are responsible for advancing the football. On defense, their main function is to prevent long touchdown passes and touchdown rushes.

Backfield. Four-member units that line up behind the line of scrimmage, both offensively and defensively. The offensive unit must line up at least one yard behind the line of scrimmage, except for the quarterback, who is allowed to accept a hand-to-hand snap from the center. Amateur units consist of a quarterback, fullback and two halfbacks. A professional unit consists of a quarterback and two running backs. One of the backs has evolved into a pass receiver, or a flanker back. The offensive unit handles the ball and tries to penetrate the defense. The defensive unit, consisting of two cornerbacks, or wingbacks, and two deep safetymen, is responsible for preventing long touchdown passes and breakaway rushes.

Backfield judge (BJ). One of six officials who polices the game, searching for infractions of the rules. His main function is to scrutinize the contest between offensive backs and receivers and the defense, checking for illegal blocks or defensive interference. He lines up to either side of the offensive backfield, 15 yards behind the line of scrimmage.

Backup quarterback. The highest-paid bench-sitter in professional sports. Usually a young player receiving on-the-job training, he plays only when the starting quarterback is in jured. However, he must be ready at all times to step into sports' most demanding position when the starting quarterback loses effectiveness due to age or injury. In most cases, he is the holder on placement attempts.

Bad hands. The phrase used to describe a prospect who has difficulty holding on to the ball, either while rushing or while catching a pass. This type of player is also called a fumbler if he manages to remain with the team.

Balanced line. The standard placement of offensive line members, in which three players line up on both sides of the center. These players are known as guards, tackles, and ends.

Balanced offense. The ability of a team to advance the ball equally as well in the air as on the ground.

Ball boy. The distributor and collector of footballs before and after games and practice. The ball boy usually is a volunteer who is a relation of a team executive or a coach.

Ball carrier. Anyone who runs with the football.

Ball control. Diabolical offensive domination of the opposing defense. Accomplished in successive bursts for yardage on the ground, it serves two purposes in the coaching quest for easy victory: (1) it consumes valuable minutes on the clock, and (2) it keeps the opposing offense on its bench, eroding its time to put points on the scoreboard.

Banana. A bending pass route used by pass receivers in an effort to split two defensive players; its path follows an in-and-out pattern along the seam of two defensive zones.

Bang. A good hit. Slang used by a coach as a blanket order to his players when they are not as aggressive as he would like them to be.

Banged up. Locker room jargon for a series of injuries which cut a player's effectiveness, but which do not prevent him from playing.

Banjo. Double-team coverage of a pass receiver by two defensive backs or by a defensive back and a linebacker; two defensive players covering one offensive receiver.

Bat. The act of knocking the ball to the ground when it is passed, punted, or place-kicked.

Belly series. An offensive system (T-formation) in which the quarterback places the ball in the stomach (belly) of a running back and rides with him into a hole. If the hole is open, he lets the running back have the ball. If it isn't, he takes the ball and either gives it to a trailing back or rushes around the end. This system is used mainly by intercollegiate, scholastic, and sandlot teams.

Bench procedure. Consists of coordination of the intelligence system and effective use of substitutions during a game. The head coach supervizes the operation, headquartered at the sideline bench. He analyzes a continual rundown of the opponent's strengths and weaknesses, fed to him by assistant coaches (spotters) located in the press box, via a telephone system. His next step is to select the proper strategy and relay it to his offensive quarterback or defensive signal-caller, usually by messenger service (sub) or by some form of sideline signal system. The most efficient intelligence network and manpower replacement system functions within a one-play time lapse.

Bench warmer. A player who spends most of the game sitting on the bench. Either he is not talented enough to play with the outcome of the game at stake or he is a newcomer with potential.

Birddog. Nickname for talent scouts in general. It applies to scouts who hunt for recruits in the high school ranks as well as to professional scouts, who find and rate the intercollegiate prospects.

Blackboard session. A period of mental cramming, during which the coaches outline vital data about their own systems or the opponent's systems on a blackboard. Modern players spend almost as much time cramming mentally as they do preparing physically.

Blackout. The ban of a television or radio broadcast in the immediate area surrounding a contest. Imposed by a governing body in control of communication rights to the game.

Blast. A reckless charge of all defensive linemen in pursuit of the opposing quarterback, with reading of the *keys* in the offensive blocking pattern.

Blind side. A player's vulnerable side, or the opposite direction from which he is looking. Two of the most harmful legal acts are the blindside block and the blindside tackle.

Blitz. A daring defensive strategy involving members of the defensive secondary, who leave their areas at the snap of the ball and charge into the offensive backfield to try to tackle the quarterback. It is done individually (safety or wingback), in tandem (safetyman and linebacker), or by the entire defensive secondary (all-out). See under *Charge*.

Block. The most essential element in an offensive attack: the legal obstruction of defensive tackling pursuit. Blocks are delivered primarily by the offensive lineman, who must dominate the line of scrimmage by driving across it, planting a shoulder in the defensive lineman's upper body and driving him away from the offensive thrust with relentless leg drive. Legal blocking requirements are as follows: In professional ball, hands must be cupped or closed, remaining inside the elbows and inside the frame of the opponent; flexed arms cannot be extended to create a push. Intercollegiate rules state that hands must be in contact with the blocker's body, and hands and arms must be held below the opponent's shoulders.

Blocked kick. The deflection or batting down of the ball after it leaves the foot of a punter or the toe of a place kicker.

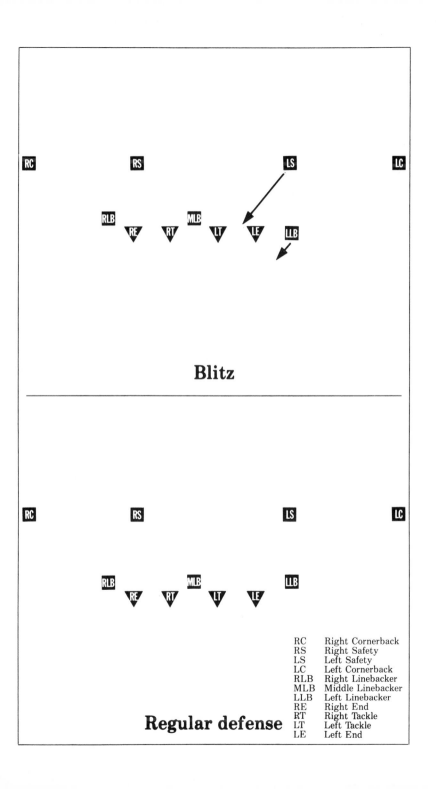

Blitz

Regular defense

RC   Right Cornerback
RS   Right Safety
LS   Left Safety
LC   Left Cornerback
RLB Right Linebacker
MLB Middle Linebacker
LLB Left Linebacker
RE   Right End
RT   Right Tackle
LT   Left Tackle
LE   Left End

Blocked out. To be driven from the point of advancement of the ball, as the result of a successful block.

Blocked pass. The deflection or batting down of a forward pass after it leaves the passer's hand.

Blocker. An offensive player who obstructs a defensive player's pursuit of a rusher, passer, or place kicker.

Blocking back. A member of the offensive backfield who blocks more than he rushes with the ball. Almost extinct, this type of back was popular before the dawn of the T-formation, but there are some variations of the modern T-formation in which he still exists, as when the upback blocks more than he rushes in the wishbone formation and the power I-formation. The old single wing offense, still used in amateur football, features the true blocking back—the quarterback—who calls the signals and blocks for the rusher on almost every play.

Blocking below the waist. General description of the cross-body block and the cut block. These methods are frequently employed by a player at a weight disadvantage, who lunges at the defensive target's sub-waistline area and makes impact with either the side of his body (cross-body block) or his shoulder (cut block). This method is not legal on a kickoff or a punt return.

Blocking from behind. A tactic in which an offensive player blocks a defender from behind at any point on the body. This move is illegal except within the three-yard neutral zone along the scrimmage line.

Bomb. A long forward pass intended to score in one thrust.

Bomb squad. Members of the specialty units, which perform such functions as kickoffs, kickoff returns, punts, punt returns, field goal attempts, and extra point attempts.

Bonus. Money that may be added to a professional contract for many reasons, such as signing of the contract itself, achieving a specified number of passes caught, passes completed, or games won, or gaining a specific amount of rushing yardage.

Bootleg. A deceptive rushing play designed for the T- formation quarterback, who fakes the ball to a rusher barreling into the line, hides the ball on his hip, and rushes around the end.

Bowed line. Deployment of the kickoff team members in the pattern of an archery bow. The place kicker lines up 10 yards from the ball, and the other members, five yards on either side, line up at lesser distances from the ball as they fill the area to the sidelines. The ends, who guard the sidelines or try to "box" the returner, are nearest to the point of the kickoff.

Bowl game. Amateur football's top post-season reward, the intercollegiate bowl often matches conference champions on an intersectional basis, but sometimes independent university teams are invited. A bowl usually involves a pleasure trip to a resort area during the Christmas and New Year holiday season and provides the competing universities with huge financial guarantees to help sustain their athletic programs.

Box formation. An obsolete offensive formation popular prior to the dawn of the T-formation in the late 1930s. The four backs lined up in a square pattern to either side of the center, depending on the direction in which they wanted to advance the ball. The tailback, who generally accepted the snap, and the fullback lined up five yards behind the line directly behind the guard and the end, respectively. The quarterback or blocking back and the wingback stood one yard off the line, behind the guard and end, respectively. It was a power system in which the three backs led one back, usually the tailback, in a manner similar to the Flying Wedge, a primitive tactic outlawed during the early 1900s because of its brutality.

Box the ends. A defensive strategy designed to stop end

sweeps. Both defensive ends penetrate directly across the line of scrimmage and wait in the offensive backfield area, forcing the rusher inside. Kickoff teams also use this strategy, instructing the ends to take without deviation a sideline course toward the point of the kickoff returner, forcing him inside toward the majority of defensive players.

Break. An unexpected happening that places a team in a hole (bad break) or in a good position (good break). Included in the "bad break" category are fumbles, intercepted passes, having kicks blocked, and bad bounces; the "good break" category comprises fumble recoveries, interceptions, and blocking a kick. Unsuccessful teams generally blame such setbacks on luck. Successful teams work at causing breaks by going over every minute detail during practice, leaving little to chance.

Breakaway. A ball carrier who has advanced beyond the deepest member of the defensive team.

Breakaway runner. A swift rusher who is capable of advancing the ball for a touchdown from any point on the field.

Breaking a tackle. A ball carrier's defeat of a tackle; overcoming or outmaneuvering the physical contact of a tackler with finesse or power.

Breaking off a pattern. Abrupt change of course by a pass receiver in order to exploit an unexpected opening in the defensive secondary created by a blitz or mental error. Deviation from the original pattern helps the passer to unload the pass earlier, thereby escaping the blitz.

Breaking the huddle. The deployment of players after a play is called in a huddle.

Broken bone. The wishbone formation version of a *misdirection* play. Two of the three backs move in one direction with the offensive line blockers, and the quarterback hands off the ball to the remaining back, who rushes in the opposite direction. It is used strictly in amateur football.

Broken play. Chaotic execution of an offensive strategy stemming from a fundamental error. The breakdown can be caused by a physical error, such as a misdirected snap from center, or a mental error, as when one rusher moves in the wrong direction. Also called a busted play.

Brokenfield runner. A rusher who is adept at eluding tacklers once he has advanced the ball beyond the line of scrimmage.

Brush block. A delaying tactic employed by an offensive blocker. He contacts a defender with his shoulder, slips off, and becomes a key blocker in a screen, a downfield blocker, or a potential pass receiver.

Buck. To carry the football into the middle of the defensive line or into the area of the majority of defensive players.

Buck lateral. An obsolete offensive play that was popular during the era of the box formation and the single wing formation. The tailback or the deep back accepted the center snap, rushed into the line, and deceptively handed off the ball to the blocking back, who turned and made a lateral pass to either of the two remaining backs, sweeping around a predetermined end.

Bulling the neck. The tightening of the neck muscles by a rusher, blocker, or tackler who is confronted with a tough situation.

Bump and run. A tactic employed by a defensive back to obstruct the pattern of a pass receiver who is moving off the line of scrimmage. The defensive back rushes up, usually blocks the potential receiver, and then turns to cover him as he continues downfield.

Buried. Said of a rusher who has been stopped by many defensive tacklers.

Burner. A player with extraordinray speed; specifically, a player who can run 100 yards in less than 10 seconds, or cover 40 yards in close to 4.4 seconds.

Busted play. See *Broken play.*

Butterflies. Nervousness experienced by a player awaiting the kickoff.

Butterfly defense. An amateur defensive alignment in which all 11 players stand upright, enabling them to have a clearer view of the development of the offensive play.

Cadence. The quarterback's signal-calling rhythm.

Call. (1) The selection of strategy by a quarterback or defensive captain. (2) The decision made by an official.

Calling the signals. (1) The selection of offensive and defensive strategy in the huddles. (2) The oral presentation of terminology at the line of scrimmage.

Calling two plays in the huddle. A time-saving strategy in which the quarterback calls two or more plays in one huddle and the team lines up in formation at the line of scrimmage immediately after the first play is whistled dead.

Canadian football. A game similar to American football except it is played on a larger field (110 yards long, 65 yards wide) with a deeper end zone. In addition, it places a greater emphasis on passing and kicking. The game is played with 12 players (an extra back), and the offensive unit has only three downs in which to make 10 yards for a first down, which causes a 2 to 1 pass ratio. There is no downfield blocking, which makes it difficult to rush with the ball, and offensive backs are allowed to move toward the line of scrimmage while signals are being called. Punt return men must advance the ball without the aid of blockers, and the punting team receives a point (*rouge*) if the opposition fails to advance the punt past its goal line.

Captain. One or more players selected by the coach or elected by a majority of the players to act as leaders.

Cardinal puff. A hazing game forced on rookies at professional training camps by veterans. Rules: the best veteran beer-drinker bottoms-up a mug of beer for each letter in the name of the game. The rookie must toast each letter and the veteran by doing the same. If the rookie fails to drink a mug in one gulp, he must start over again. Consequence: rookie's first professional load.

Carpet. Players' nickname for artificial playing surface.

Catalyst. Someone (a player or coach) who makes things happen on the field.

Catch. The reception of a thrown ball.

Center (C). The offensive lineman who snaps the ball to start a play; he is generally located in the middle of the line.

Center of gravity. A controllable point on a player's body that gives him an unbeatable impetus in the struggle for yardage. The lowering of the physical balance to this position of leverage undercuts and conquers an opponent's higher charge.

Center snap. The start of an offensive play by the center, who releases the football in an upward arc through his legs, either handing it to the quarterback or hurling it to a receiving back, punter, or holder for a place kick. Usually called, simply, a snap.

Centerfield. The middle portion of the three deep zones in the defensive secondary. This triangular area of the defensive secondary is fronted by the middle linebacker and guarded by the two deep safetymen.

Chain. Measuring marker for first-down yardage. The chain is 10 yards long.

Chain crew. See *Chain gang*.

Chain gang. Members of the unit of officials who hold the 10-yard markers. Also called the chain crew.

Championship. The ultimate achievement of a football team. The team that wins the *playoffs* is declared the championship team for that season.

Change of direction. A ball carrier's quick move in the opposite direction from which he is running.

Change of position. The switching of a player to another spot in the lineup, where his talent will be better utilized.

Character. A term describing the building of a player's courage and personality, which is often used by a losing coach trying to rationalize a negative record.

Charge. An aggressive move across the line of scrimmage by the defensive linemen and/or the linebackers (reddog) and safetymen (blitz).

Cheap shot. (1) An illegal blow with malicious intent. (2) A block or tackle made on an unsuspecting player after the ball is whistled dead.

Cheater play. Also known as the sucker trap, this offensive play is designed to exploit the aggressive pursuit of a good defensive lineman, usually a tackle. Several offensive linemen will pull toward the outside, trying to lure the defensive lineman (who is keying them) toward the outside. The quarterback hands off the ball to a running back, who runs into the hole vacated by the defensive linemen, if the "false key" is successful.

Cheating. A sneaky adjustment of position made prior to the snap of the ball by a player who is trying to get the edge on the opponent.

Check block. A delaying tactic used by offensive receivers and blockers as follows: (1) A receiver delivers an unsustained block on a defender before running a pattern. (2) An offensive blocker bumps the defender in front of him before attempting to deliver a sustained block on his primary defensive assignment.

Checkoff. An oral signal called at the line of scrimmage by the quarterback, which kills the play called in the huddle and warns the offensive unit that an *audible* will follow.

Checkthrough. A pass route run by a running back. He check-blocks a pass rusher before slipping through the guard-tackle hole, following a curved pattern in front of the middle linebacker.

Cheerleader. (1) A person (usually a young woman) who leads the cheering of the fans seated in the stands. (2) Locker room players' sarcastic term for a coach without ability or a sportswriter who sacrifices objectivity in his writing by concocting alibis for front office and coaching inadequacies.

Chin strap. A plastic strap that secures the helmet and contains a protective chin piece.

Choose the wind. To reject ball possession after winning the pre-game coin flip and to choose to defend the end of the field which puts the wind behind a team.

Chuck. A delaying tactic used by linebackers and defensive backs to prevent a pass receiver—primarily the tight end—from gaining quick clearance over the middle. The defender delivers either a forearm shiver or a hand shiver to throw the potential receiver off stride.

Circle. A circular pass route followed by a running back through the gap between the tight end and the tackle, along the seam of the strong-side defensive zone, and around the middle linebacker.

Cleats. (1) Locker room reference to footwear. (2) Plastic or hard rubber protrusions from the soles of footwear, which provides traction on natural surface.

Clinch. (1) To put the outcome of the game out of reach. (2) To gain an insurmountable lead in the race for the championship.

Clip. Illegal obstruction of a defender by a blocker. A clip is a hit from behind or from below the waist on kickoff returns and punt returns in amateur football. See also *Legal clip zone*.

Clipboard. A board on which a coach clips vital data for practice sessions and games.

Clock. Mechanical or electronic device used to time a game.

Closer look. An extended observation of a player's talent as *cutdown time* approaches.

Clothesline blow. A malicious tactic used by a defensive back or linebacker in an effort to intimidate a ball carrier or pass receiver. The tackler extends his arm to shoulder height, attempting to hit the ball carrier in the neck and chin area, knocking him backward. Illegal if deemed intentional by an official, this move carries a 15-yard penalty on the perpetrator for unnecessary roughness.

Coach. An experienced individual who teaches fundamentals to players and plots strategy for games.

Coaching film. In-depth, wide-angle motion picture of an opposing team, which is edited according to unit segments such as offensive unit, defensive unit, and specialty unit. Em phasis is placed on detail rather than artistic quality, since its main purpose is to gather intelligence.

Coast-to-coast. Describes a long run, generally for more than 50 yards.

Co-captains. Any number of leaders selected from among the team by the coaching staff or elected in a poll of the players; sometimes chosen as leaders of a specific unit, such as defensive captain or offensive captain.

Co-champions. Any number of teams that climax the season with identical league-leading records or which play to a tie in the championship game.

Coffin corner. A triangular area bounded by the goal line and the sidelines.

Coin toss. A pre-game ceremony in which the referee asks the visiting captain to call the flip of a coin to determine possession of the ball to start the game. If the visiting captain correctly calls the coin toss, he chooses either possession of the ball or the end zone he wishes to defend. The loser of the coin toss has the same option at the start of the second half.

Color man. The announcer on a radio broadcast or a telecast who provides insight into the personalities and technical aspects of the game.

Combo. (1) Collaboration between two defensive backs in coverage of two pass receivers. (2) A mixture of strategies in the defensive secondary, which incorporates zone coverage and man-to-man coverage on the same play.

Comeback. A turnabout in the trend of a game, in which the trailing team rallies to overcome a substantial point deficit.

Comeback pattern. A pass route on which a receiver sprints hard downfield, driving the defensive coverage deep, and then stops and runs back several yards.

Commit. To overreact, as on an offensive or defensive assignment. For example, when a safetyman moves up too quickly, he commits himself to an attempt to stop a rush or a short pass and allows a receiver to get behind him.

Company man. A sportswriter or front office underling who continually compliments the organization in spite of its insufficiencies.

Complementary pattern. A pass route run by receivers who are not the primary receiver, or the passer's initial target.

Completion. The reception of a forward pass.

Concealing the ball. An illegal offensive tactic that carries a 15-yard penalty. A player hides the ball under his jersey or uses a substitute, such as a helmet, in an effort to deceive the defense.

Concentration. The focus of mental energy applied by a player or a team; the stronger the level of concentration, the better the play.

Concession. A vending business that functions at major stadiums, selling food, souvenirs, and other items.

Contact. To make impact with another player.

Containment. A defensive term designating individual responsibility for turning a rusher into the center of the field and in the direction of the majority of defenders.

Continuing action. Player activity occurring after the ball is declared dead.

Continuity. A term used in coaching to describe the consistency of the offensive or the defensive unit. Winning coaches seldom use it; losing coaches often stress "the lack of continuity" as a reason for defeat.

Controlled scrimmage. Pre-season simulation of game conditions between the offensive and defensive units or against another squad. Coaches join huddles and police the action, modifying the ferocity of the physical contact and stopping the action in order to correct individual mistakes.

Conversion. The attempt to add an extra point or points after a touchdown. According to intercollegiate rules, the ball is placed on the three-yard line, and the team has the option of either place kicking in an attempt for one point or rushing or passing in an attempt for two points. In the professional game, the ball is placed on the two-yard line, and a team is awarded only one point for a successful place kick or rush and pass.

Coordinator. A coach who oversees the organization of an individual unit such as the offensive unit, defensive unit, or specialty unit. He is responsible for managing the work of the assistant coaches, the game plan, the scouting report, the teaching of fundamentals, and the game substitutions.

Corner. The area at the scrimmage line immediately outside of the end positions. In relation to field layout, it is the triangular area bounded by the sideline and the goal line or the sideline and the endline of the end zone.

Corner kick. A punt angled to roll dead or out of bounds in an area bounded by the sideline and goal line.

Corner pattern. A pass route angled toward any of the four end zone corners.

Cornerback (CB). A defensive secondary player who protects the outside flanks against rushes and covers the wide receivers on passing attempts.

Count. The signal on which the ball will be snapped, setting the offense into motion.

Count pass. A sophisticated passing maneuver involving a synchronized mental countdown between passer and receiver, which carries the pass and the receiver to a pre-designated rendezvous.

Counter play. A rushing action designed to exploit the defense's overreaction to the offense's strong-side motion. Usually, the quarterback fakes a handoff toward the strength (strong side) while actually handing off to a back who rushes toward a weak-side hole, or away from the offensive blocking motion.

Cover. The individual act of guarding a receiver as he runs the pass route.

Coverage. Coordinated defense against a pass play, involving the secondary and the linebackers.

Coverage breakdown. Disorganization in the defensive secondary or a mental blunder that permits a receiver, or receivers, to catch passes and achieve significant yardage consistently.

Crab block. An offensive lineman's attempt to trip up a tackler by lunging to the ground and using his hands and feet to push himself sideways into the opponent's leg area.

Crackback. Any legal block made by a player flanked wide (wide receiver) on the blind side of a linebacker or defensive end. In intercollegiate ranks, the block cannot be made below the waist within a three-yard zone at the scrimmage line. According to professional rules, the block cannot be made from behind.

Cradle. A fundamental pass-catching method: the receiver cups his hands and touches his elbows as if holding a baby, and softly pulls the thrown football into his chest.

Crash. Defensive strategy that sends the ends rushing directly toward the quarterback instead of reading *keys* and protecting against the outside run.

Crawling. Forward advancement of the ball by a rusher after any part of his body has touched the ground except his hands or feet. The professional rule differs from amateur regulations only in that advancement is allowed until the rusher has been contacted by a defensive player.

Creamed. Slang for having been hit savagely by one or more players.

Crisscross. An offensive backfield and pass route strategy designed to confuse the defense. The quarterback hands off the ball to a second back in a crossing action or throws to the receiver who is open after a crossing action downfield.

Cross block. A crossing action between two offensive linemen in carrying out their blocking assignments. The outside man, or man farthest from the ball, makes the first move inside; the second player steps behind for clearance, then makes his block.

Crossbar. The horizontal part of the goal post, which stands 10 feet high and is parallel to the goal line in professional ball and parallel to the end line of the end zone in intercollegiate ball.

Cross-body block. An effective blocking method used by a player who is at a weight disadvantage. He lunges off his feet, tucks his elbow into his side, makes contact with his side and hip on the opponent's lower torso, and rolls. This maneuver is an effective *downfield block*. See under *Blocking below the waist*.

Crossing pattern. A pass route that takes an outside receiver across the middle of the field, between linebacker zones and the deep safety zones.

Crossover step. A brokenfield runner's favorite escape tactic when confronted with a tackler or two. He lifts one leg high, throws it across the other leg, pivots on the planted foot in the direction which he turned the leg, and changes direction away from the tackler or tacklers with a minimum of steps.

Cup. See *Pass protection*.

Curfew. Deadline for players' return to dormitory or hotel room during training camp and road trips. Violators are fined heavily.

Curl. A pass route similar to the *comeback pattern*. The receiver drives downfield toward a defender, turns more slowly than on the comeback pattern, and then loops back toward the passer.

Cut. (1) A rusher's change of direction. (2) A blocking tactic used by offensive linemen as a diversion from the normal shoulder block. The blocker fires off line but puts his shoulder into the defender's leg area rather than into his chest, cutting the opponent off his feet. See under *Blocking below the waist*. (3) To be removed from the team's roster at *cutdown time*.

Cutback. A rusher's sudden turn upfield behind blockers.

Cutdown time. A professional club's deadline for paring down its roster to league specifications. Normally, it comes after the final pre-season game, just prior to the first game of the championship season. Also called deadline.

Danger zone. According to field position breakdown, the area between a team's own goal line and the 20-yard line is considered the most dangerous zone in which to begin an offensive series.

Daylight. Any opening or *hole* in the defensive line through which a rusher gains yardage.

Dead ball. A ball not in play, as when a kick hits the goal post and rolls back onto the field.

Deadline. See *Cutdown time*.

Deadlock. A tie in the score or a game that ends with the teams totaling an equal amount of points.

Deception. The art of hiding the ball and confusing the defense with quarterback fakes and multiple player handoffs.

Deep pattern. Any pass route that goes beyond the extremes of the defensive secondary.

Deep sideline pattern. Any pass route that goes to the deepest extremes of a defensive secondary and then is turned toward the sideline.

Defense. The 11-man unit that protects its end zone from penetration by the offense. It consists of three integral parts: the defensive line (down linemen), the linebackers, and the defensive secondarymen.

Defensive captain. The player (or players) designated by the coaches or elected by the players to call defensive signals and make decisions concerning penalties.

Defensive line game. Any strategy used by defensive linemen in an effort to confuse offensive blocking patterns. See, for example, *Loop*.

Defensive secondary. The area beyond the line of scrimmage that is vulnerable to pass completions and guarded by the linebackers, the cornerbacks and the defensive safetymen, who are known as the defensive secondarymen.

Deflection. Obstruction of a kicked or thrown ball by a player.

Delay of game. Taking an excessive amount of time putting the ball into play. The offense has 30 seconds in which to huddle and set its play in motion. Violation brings a five-yard penalty.

Delay pattern. Any pass route on which the potential receiver pauses at his position, waiting for his coverage to occupy itself with another receiver, before running into an open area.

Desire. A coaching term used to describe a player's or team's aggressiveness or lack of it.

Direct snap. The center's delivery of the ball to a player directly behind him.

Discipline. The code of physical and social practices followed by the players and enforced by the coaches or front office; the manner in which the players behave on and off the field.

Disqualified player. A player ejected from a game for any number of blatant rules infractions, foremost of which is fighting or malicious, unnecessary roughness.

Dive hole. The gap between offensive guard and tackle.

Dive play. An offensive backfield maneuver in the T- formation that is used in short yardage situations. Either of the running backs moves straight ahead, accepting a handoff from the quarterback and attempting to punch out the necessary yardage for a first down or a touchdown. Invariably, the running back hurtles headfirst into or over the line; hence the name of the play. Also called a pop.

Divide. An offensive pass play sending two running backs on sweep-and-up routes outside the tackle holes in an attempt to divide the linebacker coverage.

Division. A segment of a league, which is broken down in to geographical groups.

Dog. Blitz by an outside linebacker, who charges outside the defensive end into the offensive backfield.

Double cover. A strategy in which two defensive-secondaries guard one offensive receiver. Also called double up.

Double-dealer. A deceitful, subtle, insidious fellow; one who acts two parts at the same time; one who says one thing and thinks another.

Double dog. Blitz by both outside linebackers at the same time.

Double foul. Rules infractions by both teams, which causes a replay of the down.

Double pump. Hesitation in throwing motion of a passer who has decided to throw to another area; usually a decoy motion, but it can be a split-second decision to pass to a receiver who is a better target.

Double reverse. An offensive backfield play that develops into an exchange of the ball between two or more players. The exchanges are made parallel to and behind the line of scrimmage.

Double team. Also called a sandwich. (1) Two offensive players blocking one defensive player. (2) Two defensive-secondarymen covering one offensive receiver.

Double up. See *Double cover*.

Doublewing. An offensive backfield formation that places two receivers on each side. The variation from the normal pro set is that the weak-side set back moves into a slot between the wide receiver and the tackle.

Down-and-out. A pass route on which the receiver runs straight downfield, then breaks directly toward the sideline.

Down lineman. A defensive player who takes his position on the line of scrimmage in a three- or four-point stance.

Down-the-line blocking. An offensive procedure for a line checkoff when the defense changes at the line of scrimmage and moves into gap alignment. The offensive linemen automatically change their assignment and block the men immediately inside them toward the ball.

Down-the-middle. Describes a pass thrown into the centerfield area, generally into a heavy concentration of defensive players.

Downfield. The area beyond the line of scrimmage on the defense's end of the field.

Downfield block. A block thrown by an offensive player in the defensive secondary or beyond.

Downing the ball. A procedure in which a member of the punting team touches the punted ball, which gives the receiving team the ball at the spot it was first touched. A popular misconception is that the ball is dead at the spot; actually, the rule states that the receiving team can advance the ball after it is touched without danger of losing it, even on a fumble.

Downs. Offensive opportunities to advance the ball. A series includes four opportunities to advance the ball 10 yards for a *first down*, which entitles the offense to four more opportunities.

Draft. A professional league's organized recruitment of college talent. Drafting is generally done in a manner that gives first choice to the club or clubs with the worst won-lost record, and so on in an inverted succession.

Draft choice. A college player selected in the professional *draft*. Also called a draft pick.

Drag pattern. A tight end (or strong-side end) pass route that takes three or four steps on an angle toward the middle of the field and then moves back on an angle toward the sideline and the backfield.

Draw play. An offensive backfield maneuver exploited most efficiently by teams that pass well. The passer fades to pass but instead slips the ball into the belly of a running back, who delays and picks a hole in the defensive rush, which often overruns the ball carrier. Also called fullback draw and halfback draw.

Drive. An offensive unit's control of the ball for a succession of first downs.

Drive play. A weak-side rush by the strong-side set back, who crosses center to accept a handoff from the quarterback and rushes off the weak-side guard-tackle hole.

Drop. The retreat of a defensive player into a pass coverage zone or area.

Drop kick. An extinct method of attempting *conversions* and field goals without the aid of a holder. The kicker drops the ball as if he were punting and kicks it with his toe as it is touching the ground or after it bounces off the ground. The greatest dropkicker of all was Jim Thorpe.

Dropback. The quarterback's retreat into a protective pocket for a passing attempt.

Dummy call. A fake *audible* at the line of scrimmage, designed to confuse the defense. The quarterback yells a dead color or number, which does not change the play called in the huddle but causes the defensive alignment to adjust, often to the offense's advantage.

Dummy drill. Rehearsal of offensive plays in practice against 11 defensive men, each holding an air bag or blocking dummy. Offensive players carry out assignments as blockers simulate blocks by hitting the bags. Also called dummy scrimmage.

Dummy scrimmage. See *Dummy drill.*

Dumping it off. A passer's attempt to unload the ball when all of his receivers are covered and he is trying to avoid being thrown for a loss. This maneuver is illegal if no eligible receiver is in the area of the thrown ball. It carries a 15-yard penalty and loss of down.

Eagle 5-2-4 defense. A successful innovation in defensive football created by Eagles' coach Greasy Neale in the late 1940s that stopped popular professional offensive thrusts such as sweeps, off-tackle power plays, sideline passes, and fly patterns. It was the first pro defense to use cornerbacks in an effort to relieve pressure on the two deep safetymen. However, its weakness was in the center against trap runs and hook patterns, because there was no middle linebacker.

Earphones. Telephone headsets worn by spotters in the press box and the coach on the field who is responsible for relaying scouting information to the bench and the players on the field.

Eat the ball. A passer's act of submission to a *sack* rather than chancing a poorly-thrown pass.

Eligible pass receiver. In professional football, any member of the offensive backfield, except for the T-formation quarterback and the two players who line up at both ends of the offensive line. Intercollegiate rules are more specific because they also allow for designated numeral pass eligibility such as all members of the offensive backfield plus those members on the end of the line not wearing the numbers 50 through 79.

Encroachment. (1) A defensive player's violation of the scrimmage line neutral zone at the snap. (2) Physical contact of an offensive lineman by a defensive player or players prior to snap of ball. Penalty: five yards.

End lines. White lines running the width of the field at the back of the *end zone.*

End run. Any rush designed to go outside either offensive end.

End sweep. See *Sweep*.

End zone. An area bordered by the goal line, the end line, and the sidelines, which measures 30 by 160 feet.

End-around reverse. A behind-the-line handoff to an end by a quarterback or a running back. The end rushes with the ball or sometimes passes. An infrequently used maneuver.

Ends (E). Players who line up at each end of the offensive and defensive lines; or, the positions played by these players.

Enforcement spot. The point from which a penalty is marked off.

Equipment man. The head of the staff that distributes, collects, cleans, and reconditions equipment.

Error. Any mistake, mental or physical, that retards the progress of the offense or causes a breakdown in the defense.

Establishing a running game. The systematic destruction of a defense with the proper selection of rushing plays, effective blocking, and artful ball-carrying.

Execution. The manner in which the players coordinate their individual assignments.

Exhibition. A nonchampionship game, or one that has no bearing on the won-lost status of a team in a league race. Preseason games played for preparatory purposes fall into this category.

Expansion. Addition of new franchise in professional league.

Extra period. A fifth period, usually of 10 minutes' duration, added to professional games that are tied at the end of regulation. The first team to score is the winner, abruptly ending the game.

Extra point (EP). The opportunity to score one or (in college football) two points after a touchdown.

Eye-read. The searching of an opponent's eyes for an indication of his intended direction. A safetyman covering a wide receiver employs this technique.

Face guard. Illegal obstruction of an intended pass receiver's view by a defensive player, who places his hands or arms in the victim's line of vision. The penalty is similar to that for pass interference; 15 yards and automatic first down for the offensive team.

Face mask. Eye, nose, and mouth protector made of molded plastic or hard rubber and attached to a helmet.

Fade. (1) To retreat into a protective cup to pass (quarterback). (2) To retreat into zone defense (defensive back or linebacker).

Fair catch. Unhindered catch of a punt by a returner, who signals by placing one arm above his head (pro rule) or waves his hand above his head (collegiate rule). Members of the punting team must not touch him and must give him enough clearance to catch the ball. Interference with a fair catch attempt incurs a 15-yard penalty. In professional football, a team may attempt a free kick (unhindered field goal try) from the site of a fair catch. If successful, such a kick earns three points.

Fake. Simulated handoff by a quarterback to a running back.

Fake field goal. A surprise rush or pass out of placement formation. The ball usually is snapped to the holder, who rushes or passes, but sometimes the placekicker receives the snap and attempts a rush or pass.

Fake punt. A pass or rush out of a punt formation, usually attempted by the punter.

Fan. An avid follower of a sport or a team. This type tends to root for his or her favorite team without regard for its efficiency.

Fan pattern. A break toward the sideline simultaneously by two or three pass receivers at varying distances beyond the scrimmage line.

Feet in bounds. Legal pass reception by a receiver. He must keep a least one foot off the sideline stripe in college ball and both feet off the sideline stripe in pro ball.

Field. The playing area, which is 120 yards long and 53.3 yards wide. It is divided into 10-yard segments, and the segments at each end are known as end zones. The surface of the field is made either of natural dirt and grass or of synthetic grass.

Field goal. A placement or drop kick that originates from the scrimmage line and goes over the crossbar of the defending team's goal post from any point on the field. Result: three points.

Field judge (FJ). This referee is positioned on the defensive side of field, about 15 yards deep. He rules plays in the end zone, measures time-outs, polices the 30-second clock, governs punt receptions and defensive activity against deep receivers, and rules on field goal attempts.

Field markers. Flags or pylons implanted at intersections of the goal line and the sideline.

Field position. The point on the field where the offense puts the ball into play.

Field position zones. The four start-off areas that affect the calling of offensive plays. They are as follows: danger zone, from own goal line to 20; negative zone, from own 20 to own 40; neutral zone, from own 40 to opponent's 40; positive zone, from opponent's 40 to opponent's goal line.

Fielding the ball. The tracking down and catching of a kickoff or a punt by the return man.

Fifty-three defense. A popular professional defense that consists of three down linemen, four linebackers, and four safetymen. Developed by Miami Dolphins coach Don Shula, it derives its name from the pass coverage—five short zones and three deep zones can be covered adequately—and from the fact that the fourth linebacker was No. 53, Bob Matheson. It has been copied by many other professional clubs.

Financial adviser. An investment expert who handles professional players' financial affairs, such as negotiating contracts and making business deals.

Finesse block. An experienced blocker's use of body position and angle instead of power in obstructing a defensive player's pursuit of a ball carrier.

Fired up. Playing with a ferocious appetite for contact and a ceaseless hustle.

First down. The initial play of an offensive series; the reward for a 10-yard offensive advancement, except from inside the opponent's 10-yard line.

First down markers. Two sticks attached to either end of a 10-yard chain, used to measure distance for first down yardage.

First man downfield. The initial player on kickoff and punting units to threaten the kick or punt returner; he is usually assigned to break up the formation of a blocking wedge.

First man out of the backfield. A defensive pass coverage assignment for linebackers who are not playing zone.

First-and-goal. An offensive series commencing inside the opponent's 10-yard line.

First-stringer. The player who starts the game at a particular position.

Five-four defense. A defensive alignment consisting of five linemen, four linebackers, and two safetymen. Originated by the University of Oklahoma to stop its own Split T-Formation and option play, it is used mostly in amateur football.

Five-three defense. A solid defense used by amateur teams in passing situations. It consists of five down linemen, three linebackers, and three safetymen who can cover the three primary receivers on quick deep pass routes.

Flag. A field marker implanted at the intersections of the goal line and the sideline.

Flag pattern. Many offensive systems use the flag as a target for deep pass routes taken by their wide receivers, who run straight downfield and then angle for the flag.

Flanker (F). An offensive back who lines up outside the tight end or the strong-side end in the T-formation.

Flanks. The outside extremes of the scrimmage line.

Flare pass. A quick pass to a running back, who swings wide out of the backfield.

Flat. The backfield area located outside the ends, behind the line of scrimmage.

Flat pass. A *screen pass* or *flare pass* to a running back.

Flea-flicker. The ultimate in *razzle dazzle* offensive strategy. It involves a reverse and a lateral pass back to the T-formation quarterback, who usually throws a long pass to a wide receiver.

Flex defense. A complicated defensive alignment developed by Dallas Cowboys' coach Tom Landry. The down linemen are stationed at varying distances from the ball, which is at the scrimmage line, and the linebackers are placed in cover-up positions either behind the linemen or in the gaps between the linemen. When the ball is snapped, each defensive player moves to a lane of responsibility rather than performing in the normal "read-a-key-and-react" defensive manner. Player positioning and reaction are flexible according to down and yardage, which is one reason for its name. The other reason is that its durability has proven that it "may bend but it rarely breaks."

Flip flop. To reverse the positions of the pass receivers; for instance, to move the strong-side end and the flanker to the weak side.

Flood. To send more pass receivers into an area than there are pass defenders.

Flow. Direction in which the majority of blockers move.

Fly pattern. A straight-ahead sprint by a wide receiver, who simply tries to outrun his defensive coverage.

Flying tackle. A diving stop of a breakaway ball carrier, usually from behind.

Flying wedge. Illegal offensive strategy in which several players lock arms and form a blocking cordon for a ball carrier, running over would-be tacklers. It was ruled illegal in the first decade of the twentieth century, when President Theodore Roosevelt threatened to ban the game because of frequent fatal injuries caused by the tactic.

Fold. A cross-blocking action between the center and the guard on the rushing play into the center of the line.

Followthrough. The form of a passer, punter, or place-kicker, following release of the ball. Certain fundamental techniques are necessary in this process: a passer's over-the-head motion should continue on a downward arc after the pass is thrown; a punter's foot should continue on an upward climb above his head; and a place kicker's eyes should remain on the impact spot to assure that his head remains down as his toe swings above his head.

Football. An ellipsoid object used to play the game, made of pebble-grained leather or rubber. Professional rules specify that a leather ball must be used. Intercollegiate rules state that if both teams agree, a rubber-covered ball may be used. The ball generally is 11 to 11¼ inches long, 28 to 28½ inches in circumference, and 21¼ to 21½ inches in diameter. It usually is inflated with 13½ pounds of air and must weigh between 14 and 15 ounces.

Footing. Player traction which varies according to the type of footwear, the weather, and type of playing surface.

Footsteps. Locker room lingo for fear; a player who "hears footsteps" is considered gun shy, gutless, or shell-shocked.

Force. To prevent a rusher from turning upfield around the end.

Force man. The defensive player responsible for turning back an end sweep and making the runner cut back toward the inside and the majority of defensive players.

Forced to punt. A situation in which the offense is faced with a fourth down and long yardage. Their only choice is to punt.

Forearm lift. Tactic employed by a defensive player in an attempt to defeat a block. The defender places his forearm in the opponent's chest area beneath the shoulder pads and lifts, raising the blocker's center of gravity and breaking his momentum. It is a holding technique, designed to give the defender enought time to react in the direction toward the rusher or passer.

Forearm shiver. See *Shiver.*

Forfeit. Failure of a team to appear for a scheduled game, or malicious conduct by the home team's fans that prevents the continuance of the game. In amateur football, the offended team is awarded a 1-0 victory. The author has no knowledge of such a rule in professional football.

Formation. Any alignment of 11 players on offense and defense.

Forward pass. Any pass thrown toward the defensive goal line, even if it is thrown to a receiver behind the line of scrimmage.

Forward progress. The farthest penetration of the tip of the ball toward the defensive goal lone when the ball is declared dead.

Foul. See *Violation.*

Four-four defense. An amateur defense that consists of four down linemen, four linebackers (two outside and two inside), and three safetymen who can cover the three immediate pass receivers.

Four-point stance. The posture of a lineman as he places both hands on the surface in preparation for the snap. Originally a defensive posture, it became a popular offensive method when Darrell Royal developed the wishbone formation at the University of Texas.

Four-three defense. A basic professional defense that consists of four down linemen, three linebackers, and four safetymen. See under *Gap over* and *Gap under*.

Fragile. Locker room term for a player who is injured often.

Free agent. Any player who signs with a professional club and is not selected in the college draft.

Free ball. A live ball that is not controlled by a player, such as a fumble, a kickoff, or a forward pass. Possession is awarded to the player who gains control.

Free kick. A restricted kick, such as a kickoff or a kick after a safety, which can be made either a placement or a punt. The kicking team may not advance beyond the free kick line, and the receiving team may not advance beyond the restraining line until the kick is made.

Free kick down. A down that starts with a free kick.

Free safety. The only defensive secondary position without man-to-man responsibility. The defender lines up as the deepest man on the weak side of the secondary and is normally free to instinctively cover any downfield receiver, play the ball, or cover the first backfield man out on a pass route. In zone coverage, he guards the deep weak-side zone or the deep middle zone on a strong-side rollup.

Freeze. To cause the linebackers to hesitate before retreating into pass defense areas, thus giving pass receivers a better opportunity to beat them downfield. The offense initiates a freeze by calling a *play fake* or a *play-action* pass play, which starts with the quarterback faking a handoff to a running back.

Frequency chart. A list of an opponent's tactical tendencies compiled from scouting reports and coaching films. The chart shows the offensive plays and defensive sets used by the opponent in every down-and-distance situation.

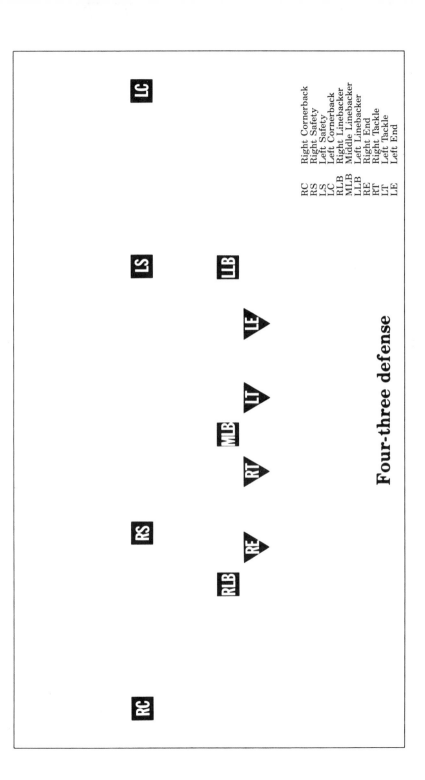

Four-three defense

RC — Right Cornerback
RS — Right Safety
LS — Left Safety
LC — Left Cornerback
RLB — Right Linebacker
MLB — Middle Linebacker
LLB — Left Linebacker
RE — Right End
RT — Right Tackle
LT — Left Tackle
LE — Left End

Fringe play. All plays involving the specialty units; an event affecting the score while the specialty units are on the field. Winning coaches consider specialty play to be as important as every other aspect of the game; losing coaches tend to write off specialty play as a hit-or-miss stroke of luck.

Fringe player. A benchsitter who barely survived the last cut; someone who rarely plays.

Front four. In professional football, the defensive linemen; the pass rushers.

Front office. The non-coaching element of an organization, which handles paperwork such as contracts and traveling arrangements.

Fullback (FB). The member of the offensive backfield who lines up the deepest and most directly behind the center according to origin. The position has evolved into a physical definition; the biggest and strongest back is described as the "fullback type" as long as he can gain yardage between tackles and block well.

Fullback draw. See *Draw play*.

Fullhouse backfield. A T-formation alignment in which three players line up side by side behind the offensive quarterback.

Fumble. To lose possession of the football accidentally, other than by voluntary kick, punt, or pass.

Fumbler. A player who frequently loses possession of the ball on a rush or after catching a pass.

Fundamentals. The basic science of performing a successful block, tackle, rush, or other game skill.

Gain. Advancement of the ball by any means without giving up possession.

Game. (1) A match between two teams, which lasts for four periods broken down into equal lengths of time according to specifications set by a sandlot, intercollegiate, or professional governing body. (2) A locker room term meaning courageous, tenacious.

Game ball. A game's top prize; possession of the ball used in a game is earned by the team that wins. Traditionally, the prize is presented to the person or people most responsible for the victory. When more than one person is awarded the prize, each is presented with a ball symbolic of the one used in the game.

Game face. Locker room expression for a solemn attitude prior to the start of the game.

Game film. A motion picture of a game, which is broken down into specified segments for coaching purposes. The film is organized according to the different elements of a team's performance, such as offensive unit, defense, etc.

Game grade. The rating of a player's game performance by the coaches, who determine from game films how many assignments were handled effectively. Grades start at 100 percent for a rare perfect performance and decrease according to assignments missed.

Game plan. Pregame offensive and defensive strategy cultivated by the coaches from scouting reports and game films of the opponent. The game plan consists of a ready list of offensive plays and defensive alignments designed efficiently to attack and contain the opponent.

Game-breaker. A player who makes the decisive play in a game; someone who frequently makes the decisive play in a game.

Gang tackle. Physical contact of a rusher or a pass receiver by more than one defensive player.

Gap. Space between the offensive linemen.

Gap eight. A short yardage defense in which six players line up in six interior offensive line gaps, two line up outside the ends, and three secondary players protect against a pass.

Gap over. A defensive alignment in which linemen fill the gaps starting on the strong side and leaving weak-side gaps unfilled. For example, in the pro *four-three defense*, the weakside tackle moves into the gap between the offensive weak guard and the center, leaving the gap between the weak guard and tackle unfilled.

Gap under. A defensive alignment in which linemen fill gaps in the offensive line starting from the weak side over toward the strong side. For example, in the pro *four-three defense*, the strong-side tackle moves into the gap between the strong-side guard and center instead of between the strongside tackle and strong-side guard.

Gear. Locker room jargon for equipment.

General manager (GM). The key man in a professional club's front office. The manager handles contract negotiations, oversees drafting and trading of players, develops promotional ideas, and makes sure that a club is profit-making and successful on the field.

"Get out of bounds". A coaching command given to a rusher or pass receiver when there is little time remaining on the clock in an effort to consume time.

Girdle. Plastic undergarment that contains sponge rubber pads to protect a player's hips and spine.

Gladiate. Locker room jargon meaning to play the game of football.

Go for broke. Offensive or defensive gamble or risk taken to turn the trend of the game in a favorable direction.

Go for it. An attempt made on the third or fourth down to gain the yardage necessary for a first down, usually by a desperate team. Occasionally, a winning team will attempt to make the difficult yardage in order to maintain possession and try to kill the time remaining on the clock.

Goal line (GL). A line separating the playing field from the end zone, which is the scoring point on a football field.

Goal line defense. A defensive alignment in which most of the players are positioned on the line of scrimmage in an effort to stop a rush for short yardage or across the goal line.

Goal line stand. A series of plays during which the defense prevents the offense from crossing its goal line from a short distance and earns possession of the ball.

Goal post. Two uprights supporting a crossbar positioned on the end line in sandlot and intercollegiate football and on the goal line in professional football. In sandlot and intercollegiate football, the goal post is 23' 4" wide; in professional football, it is 18' 6" wide. The crossbar is positioned at a height of 10 feet. Also called, simply, the post.

Goal-to-go. A series of offensive plays starting inside the opponent's 10-yard line, during which a first down cannot be made by advancing the ball.

Going without a huddle. A time-saving tactic in which the offensive team does not form a huddle but lines up in formation and receives its instructions from the quarterback, who calls the play aloud at the line of scrimmage.

Good hands. Locker room expression used to describe a player who seldom drops a pass or fumbles the ball.

Good of the game. A contract clause in professional football, which stipulates that a player must not say anything derogatory about his club or league under penalty of a fine or suspension or both.

Grabbing the face mask. Intentional seizing of an opponent's face mask. This move carries a 15-yard penalty and possible ejection from game.

Grandstand. Seating facilities surrounding a playing field.

Grandstander. A locker room expression for a show-off; a player who performs primarily to please the fans and inflate his ego.

Grant-in-aid. An official document used to bind an intercollegiate prospect to a university before matriculation. It amounts to an application for financial assistance.

Grass drill. A succession of agility exercises (performed on the ground and to the commands of the coach), which are designed to build endurance to fatigue. Players must respond immediately to the coach's orders, which are shouted within seconds of each other; for example, "Run in place!" "On your stomach!" "On your back!" "Dive for a fumble!" "Run in place!"

Green Bay Sweep. An end run utilizing the lead blocking of two pulling guards rather than one pulling guard. This *power sweep* maneuver was developed by the late Vince Lombardi during the Green Bay Packers' championship era of the 1960s.

Gridiron. Slang for football field.

Grind it out. To sustain offensive advancement by short rushing bursts.

Grip. Position of a passer's or rusher's hand on the football.

Ground gain. Yardage made by a rusher.

Ground game. Overall description of a team's rushing attack strategy.

Groupie. A fan who likes to hang around football players on campus, near the locker room, in bars, or in any social gathering place.

Guard hole. The gap between center and guard.

Guards (G). Offensive linemen who line up on both sides of the center.

Guck. Locker room jargon for a muddy playing surface.

Gun shy. A player who is reluctant to make physical contact; one who allows the fear of contact to affect his performance.

Gung ho player. A spirited player with unbridled enthusiasm, who leads a team with his mouth as well as his talents.

Gut player. A courageous player whose performance improves in critical situations; one who makes frequent big plays.

Hail-Mary pass. A desperate long pass attempted by a losing team when time is running out.

Halfback (HB). Also known as the tailback, wingback, or running back, depending on the offensive formation. Generally the fastest, most durable, most agile player. Originally there were two halfbacks in every backfield. In the evolution of the professional offensive game, one of the halfbacks became a flanker. The origin of the term stems from the halfback's early location in the backfield, halfway between the quarterback and the fullback in relation to distance behind the line of scrimmage.

Halfback draw. See *Draw play*.

Half-the-distance penalty. In any penalty assessment that would move the ball more than half the distance toward a team's goal line from the spot of the foul, the assessment shall be only half the normal distance required for that foul and no more: for example, the defensive team is on its own 20-yard line and commits a personal foul, which ordinarily carries a 15-yard penalty. However, the walk-off is only 10 yards, since the ball is only 20 yards away from the defensive team's goal line.

Halftime. Rest period between the first two periods and the third and fourth periods, the length of which varies according to the rules of the league.

Halftime show. Entertainment provided by the home team during the halftime rest period.

Hall of Fame. A museum dedicated to the immortals of football. The professional Hall of Fame is located at Canton, Ohio, and the Intercollegiate Hall of Fame is at New Brunswick, New Jersey.

Hamburger. Locker room expression for a player whose mouth is much bigger than his talents; a player or coach who shrouds his inadequacies with alibis.

Hamstring. Either of the two thick tendons that run through the rear of the upper leg. Once strained, pulled, or torn, it is the most chronic of leg injuries.

Hand shiver. A primary assault tactic employed by a defensive player. He extends his arms, tenses them, places both hands on the shoulders of a blocker, and straightens him up, taking away the offensive blocker's leverage and power.

Handoff. Delivering the ball to another player.

Hang up the cleats. Slang for retirement, giving up the game forever.

Hangtime. Elapsed time between place kicking or punting impact and the act of reception; the longer the better in order to allow the kickoff and punting unit members more time to reach the point of reception.

Hard-hitter. An aggressive player who enjoys contact and plays fearlessly.

Harness. A sponge rubber horse collar worn around the neck to prevent reinjury of pinched nerves from blocking and tackling impact.

Hashmarks. Inbound lines on the field that are used for placement of the ball whenever a play is ruled dead near the sideline. Intercollegiate rules place the white lines 53' 4" from both sidelines; professional rules place them 70' 9" from each sideline. The central location of the inbounds lines promotes more exciting professional offensive play, giving the team more room to function toward the sideline, and it also presents less difficult angles for field goal attempts.

Hatchet man. A dirty player; one whose intent is more to maim than to win, who employs malicious tactics such as clothesline blows and illegal forearm shivers. Also known as a cheap-shot artist.

Head coach. The leader of the coaching staff. He is responsible for fundamental teaching, player evaluation, development of all offensive and defensive theory, establishment of game plans, organization of all practices, and bench procedure on the day of the game.

Head fake. An effective technique used by most good ball carriers. They turn their eyes and head in one direction as they are cutting their legs in the opposite direction, thus freezing a defensive tackler.

Head job. A neurotic player with talent who never fulfills his potential due to personal problems, imaginary persecution, or inability to cope with minor injury.

Head linesman. One of five officials who police the game. In college ball, he positions himself opposite the press box and is in charge of chain gang, scrimmage line, and sideline calls. In professional ball, he takes a position on the scrimmage line opposite the line judge and handles most of the same responsibilities as his intercollegiate counterpart.

Head slap. A blow utilized by defensive linemen to confuse offensive blockers. An open-hand smack on the helmet distracts the offensive blocker long enough to allow the defensive charger to slip by in another direction. It is a legal blow as long as only one is used on any one offensive blocker.

Head tackle. A dangerous method of tackling a ball carrier, which causes neck and spine injuries. The defensive player drives his head into the chest or midsection of the ball carrier instead of into the shoulder.

Headhunter. A defensive tackler who uses an offensive ball-carrier's head as target for his impact, intent on injuring the opponent.

Headset. The telephone apparatus used by the spotters in the press box and the sideline communications director. It is worn on the head to allow them freedom to use their hands for writing notes and giving strategy signals.

Heavy traffic. Concentration of defensive players in an area.

Helmet. Protective equipment for the head, usually constructed of hard rubber or molded plastic.

Helping the runner. Pushing of the ball carrier by an offensive player in an effort to gain yardage. An illegal tactic, it incurs a 15-yard penalty in professional football and a 5-yard penalty under intercollegiate rules.

Hidden ball trick. An old offensive strategy in which players hid the ball beneath their jerseys and carried a helmet in their arms in place of the ball while another runner actually carried the ball. It is illegal according to modern rules for any player to try either of these deceitful tactics, under threat of a 15-yard penalty.

"Hike!" An oral signal used by the quarterback to start a play in motion; sometimes used as a decoy to center, according to a team's playbook terminology.

Hip pads. Protective equipment for the hips and spine; usually a padded, form-fitting undergarment connected in front by a belt. Leather shells are located on the points of the hip, on the tail bone, and in the upper thigh area.

Hip pointer. A bruised hip that causes pain when there is leg movement in the area of the injury and results in limited function of the injured side.

"Hit him in the numbers!" Popular order given by a coach to a passer who is throwing inaccurately. The number on the front of a receiver's jersey is a common target for a passer.

"Hit the corner!" Coaching command given to an offensive blocker assigned to take a defensive wingback or cornerback out of the play on an end run.

Hitch. A wide receiver and flanker pass route that goes four yards downfield with a quick inward angle toward the line of scrimmage.

"Hold the line!" Coaching and fan outcry to the defensive unit when it is in a precarious situation or is being ravaged by the offense.

Holder. The player who places the ball on a tee or on the ground for a place kicking attempt.

Holding. Illegal use of hands and arms in the disruption of an opposing player's course of action. The penalty varies according to offensive and defensive infractions. For legal blocking requirements, see under *Block*.

Hole. An opening in the defensive alignment. Officially known as the offensive rushing area.

Home field. The stadium or field used by a team for daily practice and/or its regularly scheduled non-away games.

Home field advantage. The superiority provided by a team's familiarity with the natural aspects of its own field, such as wind tendencies, sun conditions, and any unusual factors in playing surface. Also favorable for a home team is the possibility of having the majority of the fans in the stands rooting on its side.

Home team. The host team; the team that makes all arrangements and sets the time for kickoff.

Honorary captain. A nonuniformed or inactive player who represents the team along with the regular captains at the pregame coin flip. This symbolic gesture is used to reward a deserving individual for integrity or service to the team.

Hook. A tight end's block on a linebacker that prevents him from moving to the outside to stop a sweep; any screen block that obstructs a defender from outside pursuit but does not knock him off his feet.

Hook pattern. A pass-catching maneuver used by big receivers on smaller defensive players: the receiver drives hard straight downfield, stops abruptly, and turns for the pass, using his body position as a barrier between the ball and the pass defender.

Hot dog. Locker room slang for a showoff, a player who does colorful things to impress the crowd.

Huddle. Grouping of players in a tight circle between downs. Strategy is set for the following offensive or defensive play.

Hurdle. A leaping attempt by a ball carrier to avoid a tackler. In this illegal maneuver, the carrier tries to lift his feet high enough to clear a standing defensive player. Hurdling counts as a personal foul and incurs a 15-yard penalty.

Hustle. Spirited movement of a team in execution of its assignments; enthusiastic attitude of players despite unfavorable trend of game.

"Hut". Oral signal by quarterback to command the snap of the ball.

I-formation. An offensive formation in which two or three running backs line up directly behind the T-formation quarterback. In the evolution of modern offensive strategies one of the backs is now used as a wide receiver or a slot back. This method provides for a wide open passing attack as well as a powerful inside rushing game.

Illegal formation. Any offensive formation in which at least seven players do not line up on the line of scrimmage.

Illegal pass. Any pass that violates the rules. In professional football, the violations are as follows: (1) Forward pass made after possession has changed, such as on a punt or interception; penalty, five yards. (2) Second forward pass from behind line of scrimmage; penalty, loss of down. (3) Forward pass from beyond line of scrimmage; penalty, five yards and loss of down. Intercollegiate violations are: (1) Same as pro violation (1); same penalty. (2) Same as pro violation (2); penalty is five yards from spot of second pass and loss of down. (3) Same as pro violation (3); same penalty. (4) Intentional grounding or intentional throw out of bounds to save loss of yards and stop the clock; penalty is five yards from spot of pass and loss of down.

Illegal procedure. Any motion of an offensive player (except for one back who is allowed to go into motion) during the call of signals; penetration into the neutral zone before the snap by an offensive lineman who has taken a three-point stance; penalty, five yards.

Illegal snap. Any movement of the ball by the center while the signals are being called; or simulation of a snap before the actual snap.

Illegal use of hands. No offensive player is allowed to use his hands except for the ball carrier, who may use them to ward off a tackler. Defensive players are allowed to use their hands to ward off a blocker but are not allowed to grasp any offensive player except the runner or contact a blocker with the palm of the hand above the shoulders more than once. Penalty is generally 15 yards.

Impetus. Player or team force responsible for movement of the ball.

In pattern. A medium-range pass route in which a receiver runs directly downfield before breaking sharply toward the center of the field.

In the air. Any flight of the ball after a pass, punt, or a placement.

In the owner's pocket. Cynical locker room expression for a player or a media person who makes excuses for a front office that shows an obvious lack of expertise and leadership.

Inbounds. All area within the sidelines and the end lines.

Incompletion. Unsuccessful forward lateral or pass.

Indirect snap. Center's delivery of the ball to any back other than the one lined up immediately behind him.

Ineligible receiver. In professional football, the following players are not allowed to receive a pass: all linemen not lined up on the ends, the T-formation quarterback, and any eligible receiver who goes out of bounds and comes back into the playing area. In college football, ineligible pass receivers are players who wear the numbers 50 through 79 and players not on the end of the line or in the backfield. The T-formation quarterback is eligible for a pass.

Infraction. Violation of the rules.

Injured reserve. Official status for an injured player in professional ball, which rules him inactive for a certain number of games even if he becomes healthy enough to play again.

Injury list. A team's rundown of injured players.

Injury-prone. Said of a player who is frequently hurt or one who suffers noncontact injuries such as muscle pulls in practice or in games.

Inner sanctum. Executives, friends, coaches, and media persons who have privileged access to the hierarchy of a football team.

Inside game. Rushing attempts made in the holes between the two tackles.

Inside release. A tight end's immediate penetration of the inside of the defensive secondary behind the middle linebacker to gain long yardage. Such a move makes him a serious threat.

Inside-outside. The priority of pass coverage responsibility for a deep safetyman. He must defend against a receiver breaking toward the inside of his zone even if another receiver is in his zone breaking toward the outside. The priority is reversed according to the type of zone called in the defensive huddle.

Insignia. The trademark or symbol of a team, usually exhibited on the helmet or jersey.

Instant replay. Video tape rerun of a play immediately after live action has occurred.

Instinct. Inbred tendency to react properly in all aspects of the game; the natural ability to play the game well.

Instinctive player. A player who reacts successfully to football situations; one who invariably makes the big play.

Intangibles. Any integral aspect of a team that is not visible, such as mental attitude or degree of aggressiveness. A favored coaching expression used by those who cannot pinpoint a physical problem with a losing team.

Intensity. An intangible measurement of a player's or a team's degree of mental involvement in practice or a game; used mostly by losing coaches looking for complicated alibis to camouflage their own inadequacies.

Intentional grounding. An illegal forward pass intended to prevent a passer from being sacked and losing yardage. Usually called when an eligible receiver is not in the area of the pass. Penalty is 15 yards and loss of down.

Interception. Any offensive forward pass or lateral that is captured by a defensive player.

Interference. Physical obstruction of a pass receiver's attempt to catch a pass after the ball leaves the passer's hand. Penalty is first down at the spot of the foul.

Interior. The area of scrimmage line between the ends.

Intimidate. To make the opponent gun shy or afraid to play its normal game.

Isolate. To force a defensive player into a one-on-one situation.

Isolation camera. A television camera used to capture the action involving the *match-up* of an offensive star and a defensive star.

Isometrics. Tension exercises done without apparatus or with elastic cords and pulleys. They are part of a football player's muscle-building weight program.

Jam. A defensive tactic used by linebackers and cornerbacks to delay the flight of receivers away from the line of scrimmage. It is accomplished with a shoulder block or with a forearm shiver.

Jargon. Specialized language of the players, coaches, and those working with the team. Playbook terminology is also included.

Jaunt. A term used by the media, meaning a long run.

Jersey. The part of the uniform that covers the upper torso and usually bears the team's insignia and the player's number.

Jock. (1) An undergarment that supports the genitals. Also known as an athletic supporter. (2) Slang for an athlete.

Juggle the ball. To have partial control of a pass, punt, kickoff, lateral, or handoff. The player does not have total possession but the ball is being carried by his momentum.

Juke. Locker room jargon for a successful fake and cut by a ball carrier.

Jump offside. To move into the scrimmage line neutral zone before the ball is snapped. A defensive player may return to his proper position before the ball is snapped as long as he does not make contact with an opponent; an offensive player who jumps offside is penalized five yards.

Kamikaze squad. Nickname for specialty units.

Key. (1) The movements of the offensive players that guide the defensive players to their assignments. (2) A defensive player's method of determining beforehand the target area of the offense's strategy. (3) To read the movement of an offensive player before reacting.

Key play. Decisive event on a certain play; a play that turns the trend of the game.

Keyed up. Fiery, spirited, enthusiastic; hustling ceaselessly.

Kick. To strike the ball with the foot by punting or placement.

Kick the man out. A trap block on a cornerback or a linebacker, used to drive either of them toward the sideline so that the ball carrier can cut back upfield for yardage.

Kick-catch interference. See *Punt return interference.*

Kicking game. All aspects of a team's kicking units, such as the kicker, holder, punter, kickoff man, kickoff return men, kickoff return coverage, and blockers for the punter.

Kicking tee. A hard rubber or plastic cup used to elevate the football for placement attempts and kickoffs.

Kickoff. A free kick used to start the game and the second half and after any scoring series.

Kickoff return. The running back (return) of the football after the free kick that has started the game or the second half or after the opponent has scored.

Kickoff return man (*or* men). The deepest member or members of the kickoff return team, who are assigned to catch the free kick and run with it.

Kickoff team. Members of the unit that goes downfield on the free kick and pursues the kickoff return men.

Killing the clock. Any offensive or defensive strategy whose purpose is to run down the time on the clock in an effort to protect a lead; a concentrated rushing attack that eats up valuable time on the clock. Also called killing time.

Knee. Any injury to the knee joint.

Late hit. Contact made after the ball is whistled dead or after a ball carrier's forward progress is stopped but the ball has not been whistled dead.

Lateral. See *Lateral pass.*

Lateral pass. A ball thrown parallel to the line of scrimmage and any yard line. The ball is considered live if completion is not made, and possession goes to whichever team recovers it. Also called simply a lateral.

Lateral pursuit. Agility and speed of defensive linemen toward the sidelines; a defensive lineman's ability to chase a running back toward the sideline or to the opposite side of the field.

Lead. The blocker who fronts a rushing play and usually is responsible for making the key block.

Leakage. Occurs when a defensive player slips in behind the blockers to stop a rushing attempt.

Legal clip zone. The only area of the field in which an unintentional clip from behind is legal. According to professional rules, for an offensive tackle who clips another offensive tackle, the legal clip zone extends for three yards on either side of the scrimmage line. In intercollegiate football, the clip zone is the rectangular area centering on the middle linemen, extending outward for four yards and for three yards on either side of the scrimmage line.

Letter of intent. A document binding a scholastic prospect to college before he enrolls.

Ligament. A band of fibrous tissue that connects bones or cartilage. Football players are often subject to strains or tears of ligament in the knee and ankle.

Line call. An offensive lineman's *audible* in which he changes the blocking assignments of all front line blockers.

Line judge. One of six officials who govern the play of the game. He lines up at the scrimmage line, opposite the head linesman. He is in charge of keeping time, makes proper warnings concerning time, times halftime intermission, assists the head linesman in determining legality of scrimmage starts, and assists the referee in determining forward progress of play. He judges motion in the backfield and outside blocking attempts.

Line up. To get into starting positions at the beginning of the game or a play.

Linebacker (LB). A key defensive player, who usually is positioned behind the line of scrimmage, where he charges to stop a rush or retreats to stop a pass. In short yardage situations, he frequently lines up on the line; in long yardage situations, he loosens up and becomes a medium zone pass defender.

Linebacker control. Offensive strategy designed to delay the linebacker's reaction to a play. The two most successful methods of control are a quarterback's fake to a running back (*play action*) and a pass that freezes the linebacker and allows a receiver to get behind him into a clear area.

Lineman. A player who is positioned at the line of scrimmage.

Lineup. The starting 11 players on offense and defense.

Live ball. A ball that is in play; one that can be advanced or possessed.

Loading. Placing an unusually large number of offensive or defensive players in one area, making it impossible for the opponent to handle them.

Loaf of bread. Description of the football when it is being carried in an improper manner.

Locker room. Dressing quarters for players.

Locking legs. The interlocking of legs at the snap is legal only between the players adjacent to the offensive center and the defensive unit. Before the turn of the century, a formation called the Flying Wedge was formed by interlocking the legs and arms of many offensive players, creating an awesome and dangerous battering ram used to clear the way for the ball carrier.

Lonesome End. An unorthodox offensive strategy used at West Point during the 1950s in which wide receiver Bill Carpenter did not join his teammates in the huddle before each play. He remained split at all times, receiving instructions from his quarterback, who used hand signals. He ran basic pass patterns on almost every play, mesmerizing the defensive coverage. Lapses of defensive concentration allowed Carpenter to make frequent big plays.

Long man. The pass receiver assigned to make the deepest penetration into the defensive secondary.

Long yardage situation. Any down on which yardage needed for a first down exceeds the offense's ability to pick it on a rushing play.

"Look out" block. One of the game's rare traces of locker room humor is found among the offensive linemen or pass protectors. It occurs when a blocker is beaten by a defensive player, which requires him to turn and yell, "Look out!" to the passer.

Look-in pattern. A route followed by a wide receiver, flanker, and tight end, which takes them on an immediate inward angle in front of the defensive coverage. They are looking at the passer at all times because there is no set delivery spot or count; the ball may be thrown at any time.

Loop. One of the games played by defensive linemen. In this maneuver, the outside position generally slashes inside an offensive gap, and the inside position loops around the inside slash.

Loose ball. Any ball that is live; one fumbled by a rusher or dropped by a punter or holder for a placement.

Loss of down. The ultimate penalty, which is incurred when the offense is guilty of having an ineligible receiver downfield or when a passer intentionally grounds the ball. (In the latter case, the team is assessed a penalty in addition to losing a down.)

Low-keyed. Calm, confident, professional behavior on the field by a well-coached, disciplined, competent player or team.

Lycanthropy. A kind of madness, in which men have the qualities of wild beasts.

Mac. General professional term for a defensive middle linebacker.

Magician. A deceptive T-formation quarterback who hides the ball well while making fakes.

Mallard. A poorly thrown forward pass that tumbles end over end or whose flight ends with the backward end of the ball descending first.

Man blocking. An offensive line blocking pattern in which each player is assigned to handle the player directly in front of him.

Man in motion. The one offensive back who is allowed to run parallel to the line of scrimmage while the signals are being called.

Man-to-man coverage. A defensive secondary strategy in which each player is responsible for an individual pass receiver rather than for a specific area.

March. An offensive series in which many first downs are made, a great deal of time is consumed on the clock, and a score is produced.

Match-up. Interesting and important physical combat between players in head-to-head positions, such as a cornerback against a wide receiver or an offensive guard against a defensive tackle.

Measurement. Official determination of whether the offense has moved the ball the necessary yardage for a first down. The chain crew brings the *first-down markers* onto the field, and the officials judge whether any part of the ball has reached the first-down point. The offensive captain may request such a measurement any time he believes that the ball has been advanced the required yardage.

Meat factory. A university that recruits football players without regard for their grades and conducts a win-at-all-costs program, disregarding the athletes' schoolwork and physical well-being.

Media. Newspaper reporters and broadcasters who cover a team or league and report the news about practices and games to the public.

Messenger guard. The offensive lineman who relays the play selection from the coach to the quarterback. Some clubs use members of other positions to relay strategy, but Paul Brown used the guard system during the Cleveland Browns' championship dynasty in the early 1950s, making it a popular method.

Middle guard. The defensive lineman who is positioned on the line of scrimmage opposite the offensive center.

Middle linebacker (ML). A defensive player who lines up opposite the offensive center, approximately three to five yards behind the defensive line. Usually the best defensive player.

Middle lineman. The offensive or defensive player who mans the interior line positions, from tackle to tackle.

Midfield. The 50-yard line.

Mike man. In intercollegiate football, the *middle guard*; in professional ball, the *middle linebacker*.

Misdirection. An offensive rushing play in which the blocking flow is set in one direction, causing the defense to react toward the flow, and the ball carrier runs in the opposite direction of the blocking flow.

Missed assignment. A player's failure to make his block, cover his man, or control his area.

Mombo. A middle zone combination in the defensive secondary in which the free (weak-side) safety joins the tight (strong-side) safety in guarding against the deep strong-side threat of an offensive tight end and a flanker. The weak safety covers whichever receiver reaches the middle area first, leaving the strong-side safety available to combine with the strong-side cornerback in taking on the other receiver.

Momentum. A spurt of positive play by a team that has taken advantage of a good break such as a fumble recovery; a coaching intangible often used as a feeble excuse for negative play by an incompetent coach.

Monster man. A roving linebacker who can line up in any position and play the ball rather than operating with a fixed area or assignment.

Most valuable player. The outstanding performer on a team or in a league as selected by the players, coaches, or the media.

Motion. Illegal movement by any offensive player during the calling of signals—except for the one back who is allowed to move parallel to the line of scrimmage. Infraction incurs a five-yard penalty.

Mouthpiece. A soft rubber mold that is placed in the mouth over the teeth as a protection against mouth and jaw injuries.

Moves. The combination of body control, faking ability, and speed that makes a ball carrier or pass receiver difficult to stop.

Moving pocket. A moveable protective area for a passer that is formed behind the offensive tackles instead of behind the center.

Nailed. Subjected to a punisishing tackle by a rusher or any defensive opponent; on the receiving end of any vicious sack or spectacular physical contact.

Naked reverse. A handoff by a quarterback or a running back to another back or end, who runs in the opposite direction without blockers.

National Football Conference (NFC). One of the two major subdivisions of the *National Football League*.

National Football League (NFL). A professional organization comprising two conferences—the American Football Conference (AFC) and the National Football Conference (NFC)—each consisting of three divisions:

American Football Conference

Baltimore Colts
Buffalo Bills
Miami Dolphins   *Eastern Division*
New England Patriots
New York Jets

Cincinnati Bengals
Cleveland Browns
Houston Oilers
Pittsburgh Steelers

Central Division

Denver Broncos
Kansas City Chiefs
Oakland Raiders
San Diego Chargers
Seattle Sea Hawks

Western Division

National Football Conference

Dallas Cowboys
New York Giants
Philadelphia Eagles
St. Louis Cardinals
Washington Redskins

Eastern Division

Chicago Bears
Detroit Lions
Green Bay Packers
Minnesota Vikings
Tampa Bay Buccaneers

Central Division

Altanta Falcons
Los Angeles Rams
New Orleans Saints
San Francisco 49ers

Western Division

Negative writer. A media person who is unafraid to constructively criticize a football organization and is unwilling to make excuses for the players, coaches, or the football establishment.

Negative zone. An insecure field position located between a team's own 20- and 40-yard lines, dictating cautious and conservative play selection.

Neutral zone. (1) The area at the scrimmage line between opposing linemen. (2) A field position zone that begins at a team's own 40 and goes to the opponent's 40-yard line, dictating imaginative and wide-open play selection.

NFC. National Football Conference. See under *National Football League*.

NFL. See *National Football League*.

Nickel defense. Defensive strategy used in an obvious passing situation, when a faster fifth defensive back replaces a slower linebacker or defensive lineman, giving the secondary eight relatively quick men to cover the six passing-catching zones.

No place to go. Description of a rusher or a pass-catcher who is surrounded by tacklers and is desperately trying to find a way to escape.

No-cut defense. A binding agreement that a prospect must remain an official member of the squad regardless of his talent (or lack of it) for a defined period of time, with a guaranteed salary even if he does not play.

Nose guard. See *Noseman*.

Noseman. The defensive lineman who is positioned opposite the center; generally in the intercollegiate (amateur) five-man line. Also called a nose guard.

No-shows. Advance-ticket buyers and season ticketholders who do not use the tickets but remain at home to watch the game on television.

Nullify. To erase the results of a play because of a penalty and replay the down.

Number one pick. First player selected in the professional draft by a club.

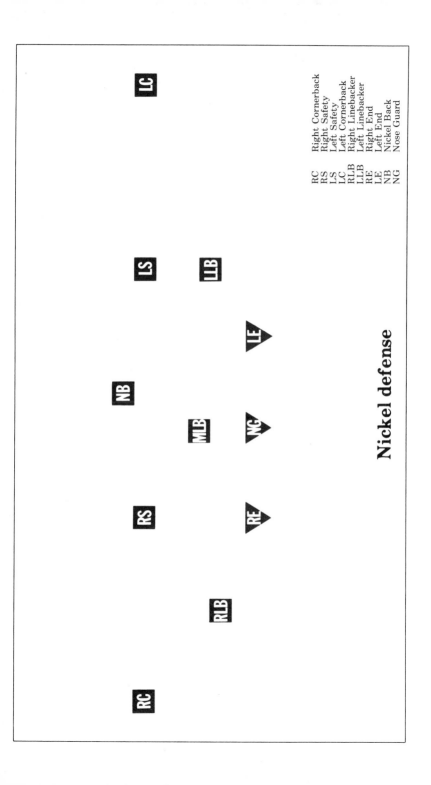

Nickel defense

RC   Right Cornerback
RS   Right Safety
LS   Left Safety
LC   Left Cornerback
RLB   Right Linebacker
LLB   Left Linebacker
RE   Right End
LE   Left End
NB   Nickel Back
NG   Nose Guard

O. Symbol on strategy diagrams for an offensive player. The symbol for a defensive player is an X.

Odd-man line. Any defensive line that has an odd number of members, one of whom often lines up head-on with the offensive center.

Odds. A betting line established by experts, which favors one club or team over another.

Offense. General term for all strategies and plays related to advancing the football; the team that possesses the ball.

Offensive line. The seven members of the offensive unit who line up at the line of scrimmage. The positions normally include a center, two guards, two tackles, and two ends.

Offensive rushing area. See *Hole*.

Official. One of six rules experts who police the game. They are the referee, the umpire, the head linesman, the line judge, the backfield judge, and the field judge.

Off-season. That part of the year when a team is working in training camp or playing a scheduled or postseason game.

Offsetting fouls. Penalties against both teams, a situation which forces a replay of the down.

Offside. A penalty incurred when any part of a player's body except the offensive center, extends beyond the ball at the line of scrimmage. On a free kick, the holder and the kicker are exempt. Penalty: five yards.

Off-tackle rush. An offensive rush between the end and the tackle.

On the ground. A reference to a rushing play; any offensive play that is not a forward, lateral, or backward pass.

On the money. Said of an accurate pass or a forward pass that reaches its target.

One on one. Man-to-man match-up between a defensive and an offensive player.

Onside kick. Attempt by the kickoff team to regain possession of the ball. If the kick travels at least 10 yards, the kicking team members may recover it and retain possession.

Open field runner. A ball carrier who is capable of going all the way once he advances beyond the line of scrimmage; one who is fast, agile, and able to break tackles or elude them once he advances beyond the line of scrimmage.

Open field tackle. The tackle of a ball carrier who has advanced beyond the line of scrimmage and is loose in the defensive secondary; the tackle from behind of a ball carrier who has broken away and seems to be heading for a touchdown.

Open up. To change the offensive strategy from conservatism to an imaginative, all-out attempt at scoring a touchdown.

Option pass. An offensive play that gives the running back the choice of rushing or passing at his own discretion; usually an end *sweep*.

Option play. An offensive system that gives the T- formation quarterback the option to rush with the ball off the tackle hole (if the defensive end plays loosely) or to pitch it out to a trailing rushing back (if the defensive end tries to tackle the quarterback, who then rushes around the end). A system used primarily in amateur football, it provides the offense with the opportunity to get around an end or linebacker, and sometimes even a defensive back, without blocking them.

Option running. See *Run to daylight*.

Option year. The 12-month period following the expiration of his contract, during which a player remains the property of a professional club and performs at a salary reduction. At the end of the period, he officially becomes a *free agent*.

Out and down. See *Out and up*.

Out and up. A pass route on which a receiver runs directly toward the sideline and then cuts sharply toward the goal line. Also called out and down.

Out of bounds. Outside the playing area, touching the sideline stripe.

Outlet man. A blocking back who swings out of the protective cup and becomes a last-resort pass receiver in case all other receivers are covered and a passer appears to be on the verge of being sacked.

Outside. Refers to any offensive thrust designed to go around the ends.

Over the hill. Said of a player who is too old, whose fading talents should be retired.

Overemphasis. Describes the corrupt policy of a high school or a university that tries to design a winning football team at all costs, disregarding the ethics, money, recruiting rules, and physical well-being of the athletes.

Overload. A strategy designed to outman the opposition in a certain area (e.g., placing three receivers on one side against two defensive backs). If the opposition does not adjust instantly, the team using the strategy gains an immediate edge.

Overrunning the play. Misjudgment on the part of a blocker or a tackler, when his course takes him beyond his assignment, causing a blocker to miss his target and a tackler to miss making the tackle.

Overthrow. A pass that is thrown too high and too hard, causing an incompletion.

Overtime. An extra period resulting from a tie score at the end of regulation in a professional football game and in amateur playoff games.

Owner. An affluent person who buys a football franchise or controls the majority of stock in a professional football organization.

Papered house. An attendance figure that has been inflated by abnormal distribution of complimentary (free) tickets.

Pass. Delivery of the ball through the air.

Pass blocker. Any offensive player who is assigned protection of the forward passer.

Pass defender. A defensive player who is assigned a specific pass receiver or a specific zone in the overall pass defense.

Pass interference. An act beyond the line of scrimmage that hinders the progress of an eligible receiver who is pursuing a thrown ball. The usual penalty is automatic first down at the spot of the foul; but if it is committed in the end zone, the offended team receives a first down on the one-yard line.

Pass protection. A unified attempt to keep defensive players away from the forward passer until he releases the pass. Also called cup and protective cup.

Pass receiver. Any offensive player eligible to catch a forward pass.

Pass rush. (1) A defensive attempt to tackle the passer before he releases a forward pass. (2) An attempt to obstruct the pass behind the line of scrimmage.

Passer. The offensive player who throws the ball to an intended receiver.

Passing situation. A second or third down play on which the amount of yardage needed for a first down appears to be more than an offense is capable of obtaining on the ground, except when the ball is positioned near the offense's goal line.

Pattern. The course taken by a pass receiver on a pass attempt.

Pay the price. (1) Trite phrase used by coaches to make players aware that victory comes only when they punish themselves beyond physical limits on the practice field. (2) A defensive theory of intimidation: make an offensive player feel pain for every yard or good play he makes.

Paydirt. Media jargon for the end zone.

Peel back. Circular retreat by a blocker or blockers in a surprising attempt to obstruct the pursuit of a tackler or tacklers in the open field.

Penalty. A forfeit incurred for violation of the rules. Common penalties are loss of down and loss of yardage.

Penalty on the last play of half or game. If a penalty is called against the defensive team on the last play of the half or game, the offensive team gets another play after time has expired.

Penetrate. To advance into the opponent's territory at the scrimmage line or in field position.

Pep pill. General term for any number of stimulants in tablet form that are used by players to induce abnormal energy and stamina.

Pep talk. An oral appeal by the coach to the players prior to a game or at halftime intermission in an attempt to inspire their performance.

Percentage call. The choosing of offensive and defensive strategy that has been successful most of the time in similar situations according to frequency charts. A low-risk decision.

Period. One of the four segments of a game; a *quarter*.

Peripheral vision. A natural gift of wide-scope vision, which enables one to perceive and assess instantly the overall situation, including developments on the perimeter of the field.

Personal foul. Malicious treatment of an individual opponent, such as striking with a fist, spearing, kneeing, kicking, piling on, or gouging the eyes. The penalty is 15 yards and possible ejection from the game.

Personnel director. The person in the professional football front office who governs the acquisition of all players. He sets up and conducts the scouting system and drafting of college prospects, signs free agents, and grades members of other clubs in preparation for possible trades.

Pick a hole. A relatively new offensive rushing theory in which a running back may select any opening in the defense instead of running directly into a pre-selected opening whether it is open or not.

Pick off. To intercept a forward pass.

Pick play. Illegal screen of a pass defender by an eligible pass receiver who makes contact physically while the ball is in the air. The penalty is nullification of the play, if successful, and 15-yard penalty against the offending team.

Picking his way. Popular media description of a ball carrier who runs under control and uses the blockers to make cuts that accumulate more yardage than expected on a play.

Picture passer. A player who uses the perfect posture, foot placement, over-the-head motion, wrist action, and downward follow-through to deliver the football to a receiver.

Pigskin. Misleading nickname for the football. The ball has never been made from the skin of a pig. It is, and always has been, made of pebble-grained leather or rubber.

Pile-up. Entanglement of many players from both teams during a rush into the interior line or as a result of pursuit of a fumble.

Piling on. Jumping or diving into a pile-up by a late- arriving player. The penalty is 15 yards.

Pill pusher. Slang for the person who dispenses salt tablets or any drugs prescribed for injured or sick players in the locker room; usually the club physician or the trainer.

Pinch. (1) A strategy used by the defensive line, in which two interior linemen are positioned in the gaps between the center and the guards and penetrate inward toward the quarterback. (2) A method of checking off a play at the line of scrimmage, in which the quarterback spots an opening in the middle of the defensive line, pinches the center to alert him of a change of plays, and runs a *quarterback sneak*, with the center as the lead blocker into the hole, into the hole in the middle of the defense.

Pit. Live contact scrimmage during practice in which an offensive lineman is matched against a defensive lineman in brutal head-to-head combat. It is generally done in the same spot on the practice field every time; this area becomes known as the Pit.

Pitch. Slang for throwing a forward pass.

Pitchout. Underhand delivery of the ball to a running back who is bellying to run around the end.

Place kick. See *Placement*.

Placement. Any kick from a fixed spot on which the ball is held by a player or propped up on a tee. Also called a place kick.

Plane of goal line. An imaginary line extending upward from the goal line, which must be penetrated by the forward progress of a ball carrier before a score is allowed.

Play. (1) A *down*. (2) A single strategic attempt by the offense to advance the ball or improve its field position, as on a punt.

Play action. A pass attempt that begins as fake to a running back into the line, with the linemen simulating rush blocking.

Play book. A team's official publication, which lists its rules, regulations, and departmentalized strategic theories and terminology. Written by the head coach and his assistants, it is considered a top-secret item, and players may incur heavy fines for losing it or revealing its contents to anyone outside the organization.

Play by play. Refers to the chronological record of the progress of a game, which is included among official statistics.

Play-by-play man. A radio or television announcer who describes the progress of a game without in-depth analysis or editorial comment.

Play fake. A feigned handoff to a running back in an effort to make a pass attempt appear to be a rushing play.

Play caller. The person who selects the offensive strategy. On the field, the quarterback usually is the play caller; on the sidelines it may be the head coach, offensive coordinator, or other member of the club.

Play selection. Choosing of an offensive strategy.

Player. Anyone eligible to compete in a game.

Player pool. Advance scouting data on college players, compiled by a central organization and distributed to a group of professional clubs in an effort to decrease the cost of scouting; a master list of professional talent composed of discarded members of each team in the league, from which expansion franchises may select a start-up squad.

Player raids. A team's or league's violation of another team's or league's contractual right to a player or players; trying to steal a player or players from another team or league by offering him more money or a more secure future.

Playoff(s). (1) A postseason game that decides a conference or league champion among those who tied for the best won-lost record during the regular season. (2) A series of postseason games involving the league's top teams in which the loser is eliminated and the surviving team is declared the champion.

Playoff berth. A spot in the postseason championship competition.

Plug. To fill a gap or hole in the defensive line.

Plunge. A rush into the interior line.

Pocket. The semicircle of blockers that protects a forward passer.

Point after. An opportunity to convert a touchdown into a seven-point thrust by kicking, passing, or rushing.

Point spread. The projected difference in points of one team's superiority over another team before the game is played.

Poll. Regional and national rating of interscholastic or inter-collegiate teams by coaches and media persons.

Pop. See *Quick opener* and *Dive play*.

Popgun. A weak passer; a quarterback who cannot throw a long forward pass with accuracy.

Pop-off. A player, coach, or employee of an organization who publically criticizes his team or superiors.

Position. Player placement in an offensive or defensive alignment.

Positive zone. The threatening field position section located between the opponent's 40 and its goal line, which gives the offense an opportunity to mix up its play selection and use its strengths to exploit the defense's weaknesses; the area within which an offense should be able to put points on the board every time.

Possession. Uncontested control of the ball by a player for a period to be judged by an official.

Post. See *Goal post*.

Post pattern. A pass route in which a receiver sets his course directly toward the goal post.

Power play. An *off-tackle rush* on which the ball carrier is led into the hole between the end and the tackle by at least two blockers.

Power runner. A ball carrier who relies on his strength and balance to break tackles and move tacklers rather than his speed and cutting ability.

Power sweep. Lead blocking by three players—a running back and two guards—on an end run.

Powerhouse. A media term for a powerful team that presents a formidable challenge in every aspect of its game.

Power-I. An amateur offensive alignment in which the three set backs are positioned in a line behind the quarterback. The offense is effective in short yardage situations, because it provides two backfield blockers for the rusher every time within the interior holes, and also is efficient on sweeps. The weakness is its passing potential, because the restricted alignment of the backs allows the defense to play tight and makes it difficult for backs to run quick pass routes.

Pregame show. Radio and television broadcasts that preview the prospective strengths and weaknesses of an upcoming game on the same station or network.

Pregame warmup. Calisthenics, exercises, and dummy drills performed by a team prior to the kickoff.

Preliminary signal. A hand motion made by the referee to the fans, benches, and press box immediately after a foul or rules violation is called. The official signal is made by the referee after the captain of the opposing team is consulted and the penalty is either refused or walked off.

Preseason drills. The tryouts and conditioning that precede the regular schedule and usually take place at an encampment where the players and coaches live without interference from their civilian lives.

Preseason game. An exhibition contest; a game that is used to judge talent and refine skills and does not count in the won-lost record.

Preseason poll. Rating of a team by the coaches and the media prior to the start of a regular season.

Press box. The stadium area that houses media people, league and team officials, coaching spotters, and scouts of future opponents, usually in an elevated section.

Pressure call. Selection of offensive or defensive strategy for a crucial play, which could determine the trend or the outcome of the game.

Pressure play. A heroic deed by a player that brings his team success on a crucial play, which could determine the outcome of the game.

Pressure player. Someone who continually makes the big play for a team.

Prevent. Defensive alignment and strategy designed to yield a short gain on a rush or pass in an attempt to concentrate on stopping a long gain or long touchdown play. Used toward the end of a half or of a game, this defensive strategy generally includes the replacement of linemen by faster pass defenders. The defenders, except for the linemen, retreat at the snap of the ball toward their own goal line to cover all passing zones.

Previous spot. Place where the last play began.

Prima donna. A player who is mishandled by the coaches, who treat him as a talent superior to all others on the team, causing a breakdown in spirit among the majority of squad members.

Primary receiver. The intended target on strategy called in the offensive huddle; the receiver chosen to exploit the defensive team's most vulnerable weakness.

Pro. An athlete who plays football for money; a professional.

Pro formation. A variation of the T-formation, in which one running back becomes a wide receiver (flanker) and is placed a few yards outside the strong-side end. There are always two set backs and a wide receiver on the weak side, the side away from the tight end and flanker.

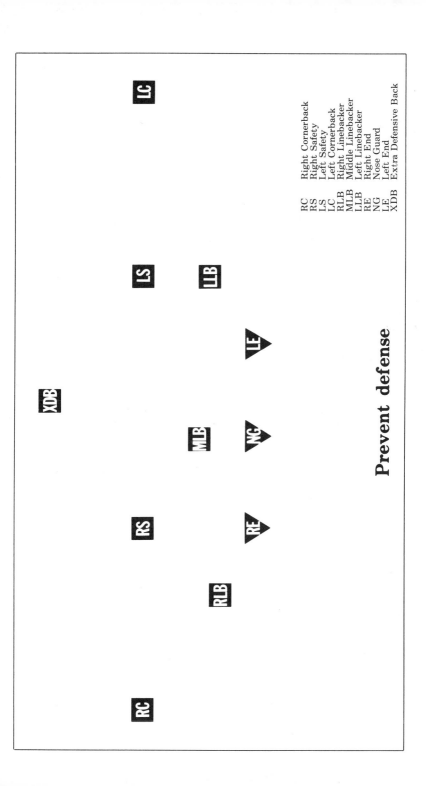

Prevent defense

RC   Right Cornerback
RS   Right Safety
LS   Left Safety
LC   Left Cornerback
RLB Right Linebacker
MLB Middle Linebacker
LLB Left Linebacker
RE   Right End
NG   Nose Guard
LE   Left End
XDB Extra Defensive Back

Pro hashmarks. Inbound lines used in professional football. They are more centrally located than the intercollegiate lines, in order to make angles for field goal attempts less difficult. Pro inbound lines are 70′9″ from each sideline; intercollegiate lines are only 53′4″ from each sideline.

Prospect. A new player with a lot of potential.

Protective cup. See *Pass protection*.

Psyched up. Playing fanatically; mentally prepared to play an aggressive game with an unusual fervor.

Pull the string. A football thrower's change of pace technique, which is used when the receiver runs a short route and the normal velocity of the pass should be decreased. A passer throws the shorter passes more softly, using wrist action and fingers to propel the ball rather than the full shoulder and arm motion.

Pulling guard. The offensive linemen located next to the center who steps back into the backfield after the ball is snapped and becomes the lead blocker in an off-tackle thrust or on a reverse or an end sweep.

Pulling lineman. Any offensive interior lineman who steps back into the backfield after the ball is snapped and becomes a lead blocker on plays designed to go around the end.

Punt. To kick the ball with the instep in an effort to gain a more advantageous field position.

Punt formation. An alignment used for punting situations: the punter is directly behind the center, seven-to-ten yards deep, and three other backs line up several yards behind the line of scrimmage as blockers. The ends generally split out, and the interior linemen usually tighten up their splits.

Punt hashmarks. Special white dot or white slash marks

placed 10′9″ outside the hashmarks on the professional football field at the 5-, 10- and 15-yard lines. The spots are used only to put the ball inbounds on fourth down so that the punter will not be kicking from behind his own goal post.

Punt return. The fielding of a punt and attempt to advance it in an effort to gain a better field position.

Punt return interference. Also known as kick-catch interference, this rule states that a member of a team that makes a punt across its scrimmage line may not in any way interfere with a player attempting to field the ball. Penalty: 15 yards from spot of foul.

Punter (P). The player who kicks the ball with his instep.

Pursuit. The flow of defensive players toward the player in control of the ball.

Push out of bounds. To physically force the player in control of the ball to step on the sideline (out of bounds), which ends his advancement of the ball.

Put out. To hustle; to play in an energetic manner.

Put points on the board. Refers to a need to score for inspirational purposes.

"Quack, quack." Sarcastic call heard on the practice field when a passer throws a poor pass that tumbles through the air like a dying duck.

Quality athlete. A prospect with every physical attribute necessary to become a star but one who never gives his coach anything else to say about him because of the coach's inability to place him in his proper position; a prospect who has excelled at many other sports and should become a fine player but never seems to fulfill his potential.

Quarter. One fourth of a regulation game; a period that ranges from 8 minutes in a kiddie game to 15 minutes in intercollegiate and professional games.

Quarterback (QB). The offensive back who chooses strategy, calls the plays, and calls the signals in all formations. After a beginning that was less than spectacular, the position has evolved into *the* most important offensive position in the game. In the old formations (single wing, double wing, etc.), the position's demands were limited, calling only for an intelligent player who could block, catch a pass, and run occasionally. In the modern T-formation, the quarterback handles the ball on every play and must be able to pass, deceptively hand off the ball, run, and act as a coach on the field. He possesses the authority to make any personnel adjustment or strategy change he deems necessary to the success of the offense.

Quarterback draw. A delayed rushing play by the quarterback, who takes the ball from center, fades to feign a pass, searches for a hole between the two tackles, and rushes with the ball through the hole he chooses. Similar to the fullback *draw play*.

Quarterback in motion. A rarely used offensive strategy which legally transforms the T-formation into a single wing or double wing formation, according to the direction of the motion. The quarterback leaves his position behind center as the signals are being called and runs parallel to the line of scrimmage, becoming an eligible receiver under both intercollegiate and professional rules.

Quarterback keeper. A T-formation sweep by the quarterback, who either rolls out around the end behind a pocket of blockers or fakes to a running back and rushes around the end.

Quarterback sneak. A short yardage plunge by the quarterback, who lowers his head after taking the center snap and follows either his center or his guards straight ahead.

Quick count. A sneak attack by the offensive unit. They break huddle and poise at the line of scrimmage for a mandatory second, but the ball is snapped before the linemen take their basic crouching stance.

Quick feet. Descriptive expression for agility rather than speed; used to praise a lineman's ability to change direction and avoid contact and a back's ability to avoid tacklers or stay close to a speedy receiver in the defensive secondary.

Quick hitter. An offensive rushing play that reaches a hole quickly and directly.

Quick kick. A punt on any down except the fourth that is made out of a normal formation and followed by a post-snap adjustment. The adjustment usually takes the form of either a retreat from the fullback position by the punter, who takes a direct snap, or a lateral from the quarterback to the punter, who has moved out of the fullback position. If blocked, the punting team does not lose possession as long as one of its members recovers the ball. The punting team still possesses any downs remaining in the series.

Quick opener. A direct rush by a running back into one of the holes in the interior line. Also called a pop.

Quick out route. A short sideline pattern taken by a wide receiver, who drives four to six yards downfield and cuts quickly toward the sideline.

Quick release. A passer's trigger sharpness; his ability to deliver an accurate pass in any range, from any position, under any conditions. Generally, this extraordinary passing touch stems from powerful wrist action.

Quick trap. An interior line offensive counterattack against a defensive lineman who cannot be handled by orthodox blocking methods (man for man, or X-block). The ball is given quickly to the rusher, who slips behind, pulling with him a guard, who crosses center to the opposite side, thus obstructing or knocking down the unsuspecting, troublesome, penetrating defensive lineman.

Quick whistle. Premature blow of the whistle by an official before the action is legally complete, such as before a rusher has reached the farthest point of progress or before a legal fumble. The rules cover most situations, rewarding a replay of the down to the violated team, but some situations are governed by the official's judgment, and the damage cannot be repaired.

Raised arm technique. A defensive player's fundamental method of controlling a blocker or fighting off a block: he thrusts both arms forward, placing his hands on the blocker's shoulders, keeping the blocker at arm's length as he angles for the ball carrier, and then he tries to throw the blocker aside as he penetrates toward the rusher or passer.

Range. The area a defensive player can cover on a play.

Rankings. See *Ratings*.

Ratings. A listing of teams, regionally and nationally, according to their strength and based on a poll of media persons and coaches. Also called rankings.

Razzle dazzle. Fancy or unorthodox offensive strategy, such as multiple reverses, reverse passes, or fake punt-passes.

Read and react. A basic defensive concept: determining where the *keys* and offensive flow are going before getting to the area to make the tackle or defend against a pass.

Reading the defense. Predetermination of the offensive strategy by watching the blocking *keys* and the flow of the play after the snap.

Ready list. A priority listing of offensive plays and defensive strategy that the coaching staff believes will be effective against the opponent.

Receiver. A player who catches a forward pass.

Receiver tree. The total number of different pass routes taken by one receiver.

Receiving team. The team that fields and returns a kickoff and a punt.

Reception. Catching a forward pass.

Record. A list of a team's wins, losses, and ties.

Recover. (1) To gain control of a free ball. (2) To regain balance after stumbling or slipping. (3) To overcome a block or a fake and make a successful defensive play.

Reddog. A *blitz* by all three linebackers.

Referee (R). The most authoritative of the six officials who police a game. He has the final word on control and general supervision of the game when disagreement exists. He lines up behind the deepest offensive back and is responsible for the coin toss, blowing the whistle on kickoffs, notifying coaches of the timeout quota and two-minute warning, and overseeing the legality of the offensive backfield action.

Regular season. An advance schedule of games that count in the championship standings.

Reject. A discard; a player who is picked up by a team and succeeds after having been released by another team or teams.

Release. (1) A *cut* by a team. (2) To deliver a forward pass. (3) To check or shoulder block a potential receiver and force him to go in a certain direction downfield.

Reserve. (1) A substitute player. (2) A player who is legally contracted but is not on a professional club's playing roster.

Retread. A veteran player who is trying to make a comeback after leg surgery; a star who has made a successful comeback.

Return. Advancement of a punt, kickoff, or interception.

Return man. A player who advances a kickoff and a punt.

Reverse. A handoff from a back going in one direction to a player going in the opposite direction.

Reverse forward pass. A pass attempt by a ball carrier who has been handed the ball by a player going in the opposite direction.

Reverse spin. An incorrect pivot by a T-formation quarterback. He turns in the opposite direction from which the handoff will be made after he takes the snap from the center.

Ride series. A system of offensive plays in which the T- formation quarterback places the ball in a running back's stomach, maintains possession as he rides several steps toward the hole, and then either gives the ball to the back if the hole is open or keeps it and runs around the end if the hole is not open.

Rifle. A forward passer with a strong arm who can throw the ball long and hard.

Ringer. A term used in amateur football for an ineligible player who plays in a game.

Roll up. To overshift the deep defensive backs toward one side of the offensive alignment in preparation for zoning the pass receivers.

Rollout. A T-formation quarterback's following of the flow of the blockers toward the outside with the option to pass or rush.

Romp. To win by a wide margin; an easy game.

Rookie. A first-year player or coach.

Rookie hazing. A series of practical jokes and pranks played by the veterans on players at their first professional football training camp.

Roster. The official listing of all eligible players and important information concerning their physical capacities and careers.

Rotation. A presnap shift of all defensive backs toward one side of the offensive alignment in anticipation of a pass to the receivers in that area.

Rouge. A Canadian football scoring rule, which gives the punting team one point if the return man fails to advance the ball out of his own end zone.

Roughing the kicker. Blocking or tackling of a punter or place kicker before he regains his balance after kicking. Such moves are illegal unless the block or tackle occurs after the ball is blocked or deflected or the contact is caused by the kicker's motion. Penalty: in pro ball, 15 yards from the line of scrimmage and automatic first down; in college ball, 15 yards from the line of scrimmage but no first down.

Roughing the passer. Execution of avoidable physical contact with a forward passer who has released the ball and is standing still or fading. The passer is protected from contact until the flight of the ball ends or he becomes a defensive player, as on an interception. The referee is responsible for judgment on this penalty, which is 15 yards from the previous snap and possible ejection if the violation is flagrant.

Rout. To win by a big point spread; a one-sided game.

Route. The receiver's course downfield on a pass attempt.

Rover. A defensive back or linebacker who has no definite responsibility but lines up anywhere he deems necessary to play the ball.

Rule blocking. A substitute blocking pattern for offensive linemen who face a different defensive alignment than the one anticipated in the huddle. In such situations, the contingency blocking plan generally requires the blocker to handle the defensive player inside of him.

Rules. Laws governing the conduct of a game.

Run support. Designation of a defensive back and/or linebacker as the containment man or men against a rushing play when the rest of the defensive secondarymen are setting up against a possible pass.

Run to daylight. To rush into any open hole instead of into a pre-determined area that may be clogged with defensive players. Also called option running.

Running back (RB). An offensive back who lines up from three to five yards behind the line of scrimmage. His major functions are to rush with the ball and block.

Running game. A general expression for every aspect of a team's rushing attack, including play calling, deceptive hand-offs, blocking execution, and ball carrying.

Running into the kicker. Inadvertent contact by a defensive player with a punter or place kicker. To run into the kicker is considered a violation in professional football only, and it carries a five-yard penalty.

Running the ball. Advancing the ball by running with it; *rushing*.

Rushing. Advancing the ball on the ground, by running with it.

Sack. To tackle the passer before he releases the ball.

Safety. A two-point scoring play for the defensive unit that occurs when it stops the offense from advancing the ball out of its own end zone or when the offense forces the ball to be declared dead behind its own goal line.

Safety valve. A blocking back who slips into flat terrain and becomes a receiver when all receivers are covered and it appears as though the forward passer will be sacked. The short pass route taken by the blocking back is designed to take pressure off a harassed passer.

Safetyman (S). The deepest defensive back: the player in the last line of defense.

Sally Rand. What oldtimers called a *naked reverse* out of respect for one of the world's most famous striptease artists.

Sam. Play-book term for the strong-side linebacker.

Sandwich. See *Double team*.

Scat back. A small ball carrier with awesome speed and deceptive moves.

Scissors. A crossing action between blockers; a wide crossing action between running backs, one of whom accepts a handoff from the quarterback.

Scoreboard. A stadium structure on which the score is posted, either electronically or manually.

Scoreless. Pointless, unable to score points; the condition of being without points.

Scout. (1) A representative of a football organization who searches for talent or prospects. (2) A coach who attends the game of a future opponent in order to record characteristics of the team for the purpose of devising a game plan.

Scramble. Movement by a forward passer away from his protective cup in an effort to escape defensive rushers and to give his receivers more time to find an opening in the defensive secondary.

Scrambler. A forward passer who frequently leaves the protective cup to give his receivers more time to find an opening in the defensive secondary.

Screen pass. An offensive counterattack against a fierce pass rush: a quarterback fades to pass; the offensive linemen brushblock the defensive linemen, allowing them to freely pursue the passer, and then set up a blocking line to either side; a running back sets up behind the blocking line; and the quarterback throws a short pass to the running back, who follows the blockers upfield, usually against an isolated linebacker, who is outnumbered by the blockers.

Scrimmage. A practice game within a team or against another team, which includes physical contact and simulates game conditions but is not officially counted on the record.

Scrimmage line. The area extending outward from the forward tip of the football to both sidelines.

Seal off. Action of an offensive blocker who takes an advantageous body position against a defensive player in order to secure an open area or lane for a ball carrier.

Seam. An imaginary line bordering two defensive zones, which splits and confuses the defensive-secondarymen when used as a route by a receiver.

Second effort. A play attempted out of sheer hustle; ceaseless determination to make a play despite obstacles; getting up off the ground to make a good play.

Second string. Backup players for every position; reserves, substitutes.

Secondary receiver. The second receiver on a passer's priority list for a passing attempt.

Seeksorrow. One who contrives to give himself vexation.

Sellout. Sale of every seat in the stadium; capacity crowd.

Series of downs. Four offensive plays that constitute a team's chance to advance the ball at least 10 yards. If they succeed, they are awarded another series of downs.

Set. (1) Positioning of offensive running backs. (2) The quarterback's oral signal alerting the unit to take a stance and await the signal for the snap of the ball.

Set back. An offensive back who lines up behind the quarterback.

Setback. An obstacle; anything that slows a team's progress; a term used by the media to mean defeat.

Setting up. Positioning the body to perform a function such as pass, pass block, or return a punt.

Seven on seven. A dummy passing drill conducted by professional clubs in an. effort to sharpen the passing game in practice. It matches seven offensive players (quarterback, two set backs, two wide receivers, strong-side end, and center) against seven defensive players (three linebackers, two cornerbacks, and two deep safetymen).

Shank. Poor contact by a kicker with the ball, usually made with the side of the foot by a punter.

Shield. A block by a wide receiver on a cornerback; similar to a *crackback* block.

Shift. Coordinated change of positioning by more than one player prior to the snap of the ball.

Shifty. Said of a ball carrier who relies more on his cutting ability than his speed.

Shiver. A forearm blow delivered in swinging fashion to the chest area or shoulder pad area of an opposing player. A legal technique used either to fight off a blocker or by a blocker to freeze a defensive player. Also called forearm shiver.

Shoestring catch. A forward pass that is caught just before it hits the ground.

Shoestring tackle. Knocking a ball carrier down by grasping his ankles or feet.

Shoot. A play-action pass route for a running back. He drives at a linebacker, feigning a block, and then slips parallel to the line of scrimmage toward the sideline.

Shoot the gaps. Coordinated penetrating action by the defensive linemen and linebacker into the gaps between the offensive linemen.

Short of time. Having only seconds remaining on the clock; usually said when a team has a long way to go for a score and little time remaining on the clock.

Short punt formation. Term used in amateur football to describe the *A-formation*.

Short yardage. Three yards or less needed for the offense to make a first down.

Short-hopping. Fielding a punt or a kickoff as it bounces on the ground.

Shotgun. An old offensive passing formation popularized by the Dallas Cowboys recently. The quarterback lines up 4½ yards deep and accepts a direct snap from the center, giving him more time to watch pass patterns progress. Very few rushing plays are successful out of it in professional ball, but it provides a wide assortment of passing possibilities.

Shoulder tackle. A basic technique taught to defensive players, who must plant one shoulder into the midsection or upper legs of a ball carrier and drive through with leg power.

Showboat. A hot dog; a player who shows off, does strange things just to catch the attention of the crowd or media.

Shuttle pass. A short pass behind the line of scrimmage, delivered with either an overhand or an underhand motion.

Sidelines. The lines bordering the playing area on each side of the field.

Sideline pattern. A bending pass route on which the wide receivers fly upfield once they've reached the sideline, confusing the defenders in zone coverage and finding an open area at the seam of the medium and the deep zones.

Sidewinder. A forward passer who has a sidearm delivery.

Signals. A series of oral terms and numbers describing the upcoming plays, shouted by the quarterback at the line of scrimmage.

Single wing. An ancient power formation in which two guards are placed on the same side of the center, creating an unbalanced line. All four backs are lined up on the same side at varying distances behind the line: tailback, five yards deep behind the center; fullback, three yards deep behind the guard; quarterback or blocking back, one yard deep behind the tackle; and wingback, a yard deep and a yard outside the end. The center usually makes a direct snap to the tailback, whose most

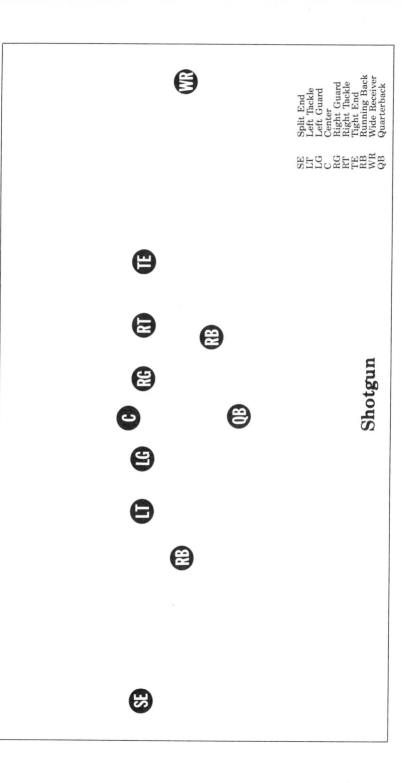

Shotgun

SE — Split End
LT — Left Tackle
LG — Left Guard
C — Center
RG — Right Guard
RT — Right Tackle
TE — Tight End
RB — Running Back
WR — Wide Receiver
QB — Quarterback

profitable play is to rush off tackle (between his tackle and end) with double-team blocks on the defensive tackle and end.

Six-three defense. A popular amateur defense, which includes six defensive linemen, three linebackers, and two safetymen.

Sixty-minute man. An extinct expression that described a player who played both offensively and defensively.

Skull session. A cram period during which the coach outlines play-book strategy for the players, reveals grades of past performances, and relays intelligence about future opponents. Usually the team is broken down into individual units for this study period.

Slant. A running back's direct angle toward the hole between tackle and end, which is usually the defensive alignment's most vulnerable area.

Slant-in. A pass route for a wide receiver. He drives four to six yards directly at the defensive cornerback and then angles toward the open area between the deep safetymen.

Slash. (1) In amateur ball, this term means that the defensive end in a five-man front runs over the outside shoulder of the offensive end, delaying his break from the line, and bears down on the fullback. (2) In professional ball, it means that the defensive end and tackle try to penetrate through the same gap in the offensive line.

Sleeper. A surprising talent discovery; a prospect who makes it big without an advance buildup.

Sleeper play. An illegal pass play, which has occasionally avoided detection by the officials and won games in past. It usually involves a deceitful substitution; for example, during a change of possession, only 10 offensive players run onto the field as 11 defensive players go to the bench. Without a huddle, the defensive unit lines up, and the eleventh defensive player sneaks off the bench and takes a set position a few yards inbounds without detection by the defense. The "sleeper" runs uncovered downfield and the quarterback throws the ball to him for a touchdown. The penalty is for an illegal forward pass—five yards and loss of down.

Slip. (1) To lose one's balance on a wet or icy field. (2) To avoid a block or tackle.

Slither. To run with uncanny body control through a crowd of players.

Slot. The gap between the wide receiver and the weak-side tackle.

Slot back (SB). An offensive back who lines up in the gap between the wide receiver and weak-side tackle; or a wide receiver who lines up in the gap between the other wide receiver and the weak-side tackle.

Smoke. To run fast; to turn on the speed.

Snake. To cut with agility behind seal-off blocks to gain an unexpected abundance of yardage.

Snap. See *Center snap*.

Sneak. A short yardage plunge by the quarterback, who lowers his head and rushes into the center of the line.

Soccer-style kicker. A place kicker who approaches the ball from the side and makes impact with the side and instep of his foot rather than the toe.

Soft spot. The best impact area on a football for a place kicker. Ideally, he should make contact with his toe just below the middle of the ball. Also called the sweet spot.

Soft touch. Smooth throwing motion of an accurate forward passer.

Spear. To drive the helmet into an opponent on a block or tackle after his momentum has stopped.

Specialist. A player who is used only for a particular job, such as a punter or place kicker.

Specialty team. A unit that performs a particular function, such as kickoffs, kickoff returns, punts, punt returns, field goal attempts, etc.

Spike. To slam down the ball after scoring a touchdown or making a big play.

Spiral. The spin of the football on a pass or punt.

Splatter. A term and maneuver originated by the great Jim Brown, who always terminated an end sweep against a hard-tackling cornerback by cutting back against the grain through the tackle hole.

Split. The gap between two linemen.

Split end (SE). An end who lines up at least six yards from the tackle.

Split T-formation. A variation of the T-formation in which the linemen are positioned farther apart than normal, causing the defensive players to leave wider gaps in the defensive line. The formation gives the offensive linemen better angles to make their blocks. Developed in the early 1950s, the formation spawned the quarterback *option play*.

Spot pass. A forward pass thrown to a spot on the field rather than to a specified receiver when he gains a clear area. The pass is usually thrown before the intended receiver makes his cut to the spot.

Spot player. A player who is used only in specific circumstances, when a particular skill is called for in a critical situation.

Spotter. A media person stationed on the field who informs the play-by-play man which players are making the plays.

Spread formation. A variation of the T-formation, which places a running back in the slot between the weak-side end and tackle and the other running back in a slot between the strong-side end and tackle. A zone-breaker, the formation gives the offense a double wing to the weak side and a triple wing to the strong side, or five receivers who can move quickly.

Spring practice. Intercollegiate football drills during the spring months, which have been outlawed in some leagues and at some independent universities.

Sprint draw. A modernized version of the old reliable *draw play*. The T-formation quarterback sprints immediately toward the end, feigning a quick pass play, and then hands the ball off to the deep back in the I-formation, who meets him at the tackle hole. The ball carrier has the option to rush outside or inside, picking the open hole. The play was made popular by the University of Pittsburgh's Tony Dorsett.

Sprintout. A series of T-formation plays in which the quarterback sprints immediately toward the end and fires quick passes, hoping to isolate a wide receiver, linebacker, or cornerback.

Squad. All the players on the team.

Square base. Fundamental foot positioning for an offensive lineman, who must brace himself by planting both feet even with the width of his shoulders when a defensive rusher attacks him.

Squareout. A receiver route on which the receiver drives straight downfield for 10 yards before sharply cutting toward the sideline. The comparable long pattern is called a *squareout and down*.

Squareout and down. A long version of the squareout. The receiver drives straight downfield, cuts sharply toward the sideline for five yards, and then turns sharply upfield on a *fly pattern*.

Squibber. A bouncing kickoff that is intentionally shanked to make the blockers return the ball and prevent a long kickoff return by the return men.

SRO. Abbreviation for Standing Room Only. Refers to a stadium in which all the seats have been sold.

Stack defense. A defensive alignment in which the linebackers line up directly behind the defensive linemen, confusing the offensive blockers. The "hidden" positions of the linebackers make it difficult for the blockers to prejudge the direction in which the linebackers will react.

Stadium. The structure that houses the playing field. Contains the seats, ticket office, and concession stands.

Stalemate. Media term used to describe a tie game.

Standard player contract. A common professional contract used throughout the leagues.

Starter. The player who opens the game in a particular position.

Statistics. A mathematical account of a game in terms of yardage and all phases of the opponents' offensive and defensive efficiency.

Statue of Liberty. An almost extinct offensive play, which is named after the famous statue in New York Harbor because the quarterback retreats to the passing pocket, starts his passing motion, and stops with the ball raised high in the position of the statue. He allows a running back to take it and sweep the end around the defensive rush that was attracted by the fake pass.

Staying home. Maintaining a position to defend an area of responsibility, and not being lured out of position by an offensive fake.

"Stick 'em!" An emotional cry imploring the players to hit hard, usually uttered by a coach or captain.

Stickum. Manufactured powder used by running backs and pass receivers to make hands sticky for a better grip on the ball.

Stiff. A bad player, a player who cannot do the job.

Stiff-arm. Extension of the free arm by a ball carrier to ward off a tackler. Also known as a straight-arm.

Stone. A defensive safetyman who takes it upon himself to leave a pass zone and penetrate as a containment man against the rush.

Stood up. Describes a defensive lineman who has been overpowered by the block of an offensive player. The offensive player has driven the aggressiveness out of the attacker.

Stop and go. A maneuver by the pass receiver. He drives straight downfield and hooks, luring the defensive back to his area, then spins around and angles out or in or tries to fly past the suckered defender toward the goal line.

Stopped dead. Made no gain; terminated an offensive thrust short of the necessary yardage.

Straddling the sideline. (1) Rushing along the sideline and keeping the feet inbounds. (2) Catching a pass along the sideline and keeping the feet inbounds.

Straight arm. See *Stiff-arm*.

Straightaway runner. A power rusher who lacks agility and cutting ability but runs over players on inside thrusts.

String it out. A tactic used by a defensive end or outside linebacker that makes them responsible for maintaining an outside position against the blocking flow of an end sweep despite all obstacles, and forces the rusher back toward the inside and the majority of defensive players.

Strip. A sacrificial act by a defensive player, who throws himself at a blocker or blockers, stripping the rusher of all protection.

Strong side. The side of the offensive center that has more players than the other side. In the T-formation, the side with the tight end is the strong side.

Stunt. A defensive line play that coordinates any action between two players other than the orthodox straight-ahead penetration.

Stutter step. A delay movement by a running back or receiver. He begins the step in one direction, hesitates, and then cuts in another direction to clear a tackler or defensive coverage.

Submarine. A low thrust by a defensive player through the legs of the offensive linemen, or through the gaps, in an attempt to catch a rusher behind the line of scrimmage.

Substitute. A replacement, reserve, or second-stringer.

Suck in. To lure a defensive player away from his responsibility or make him commit himself foolishly.

Sucker trap. See *Cheater play*.

Sudden death. An extra period to break a tie score at the end of regulation. The first team that scores is the winner.

Suicide bootleg. A dangerous maneuver by the T-formation quarterback, who fakes a handoff to a running back following all the blockers one way, hides the ball on his hip, and runs around the opposite end without any blockers.

Superstar. A player who can do it all at his position; one who is capable of breaking a game open all by himself.

Sweep. A rush around the end with lead blocking. Also called an end sweep.

Sweet spot. See *Soft spot*.

Swing man. A running back who runs a *swing pass* pattern.

Swing pass. A forward pass to a running back who is circling out of the backfield.

Tackle (T). (1) To stop the forward progress of the ball carrier with the shoulder, arms, body, or hands. (2) An interior offensive and defensive line position. The offensive location is between the guard and the end. The defensive location is opposite the offensive guard or center (pro) or opposite the offensive guard or tackle (amateur).

Tackle hole. The gap between offensive tackle and end.

Tailback (TB). The deepest offensive back in most formations; generally the best rusher.

Tampering. Trying to gain the services of a player who is under contract to another professional club.

Taxi squad. Players who are contracted to a professional club and practice with the team but are not on the official roster. They can be activated at any time.

Team. Generally refers to the 11 players on the field. Overall, refers to the entire roster.

Team doctor. The physician who travels with the team to diagnose and treat injuries on the field during practice and games.

Team manager. In amateur football, the volunteer who distributes and collects balls and miscellaneous equipment such as tees and undergarments.

Team player. An unselfish player who sacrifices personal glory for the benefit of team unity and success.

Tee. The hard rubber or plastic cup on which the football is propped for placement kicking.

Tee up. To prop the ball up for a placement kick.

Teed-off. Hell-bent on one mission, as when a defensive lineman ignores every aspect of his responsibilities except knocking down the passer in an obvious passing situation.

Telegraphing. Pre-snap revelation of (a) the direction of an offensive play, such as by an inadvertent glance by a player, or (b) of the offensive strategy, such as the lean of a lineman in his stance who is overanxiously anticipating a retreat to block for a passing attempt.

Tendency. A team's habitual choice of strategy in certain situations.

Tendency chart. See *Frequency chart*.

Tendinitis. Inflammation of a tendon, a common ailment for football players. Tendons of the ankle and knee are especially vulnerable.

Tennis elbow. Inflammation of an elbow tendon, suffered mainly by forward passers in their throwing arms, because of the passing motion.

Terminology. Coded language used by a team in its play book.

Tertiary receiver. The third receiver on a forward passer's priority list for a passing play.

T-formation. An offensive formation in which the quarterback stands directly behind the center and accepts a handoff. The fullback lines up 3½ yards behind the quarterback, flanked by the two halfbacks, giving the formation the appearance of a T. The modern formation has evolved into an alignment of two set backs (a halfback and a fullback), with one of the halfbacks set outside the tight end as a flanker.

Thigh pad. A plastic pad covered with sponge rubber, which fits into a pocket inside the legs of football pants and protects the thighs.

Third down conversion. Making the required yardage for a first down on a third down attempt.

Third down situation. Any third down play on which there is yardage to be gained in order to record a first down.

Thirty second clock. A timepiece in the end zones in professional games which shows the offense how much time is remaining to start a play before a violation is called. In amateur ball, the referee uses a stopwatch to keep track of the 25 seconds allotted to the offense for huddling and putting the ball in play.

Three-four defense. An alignment used in professional ball when the defense is facing an obvious passing attempt. The defense includes three down-linemen, four linebackers, and four defensive backs.

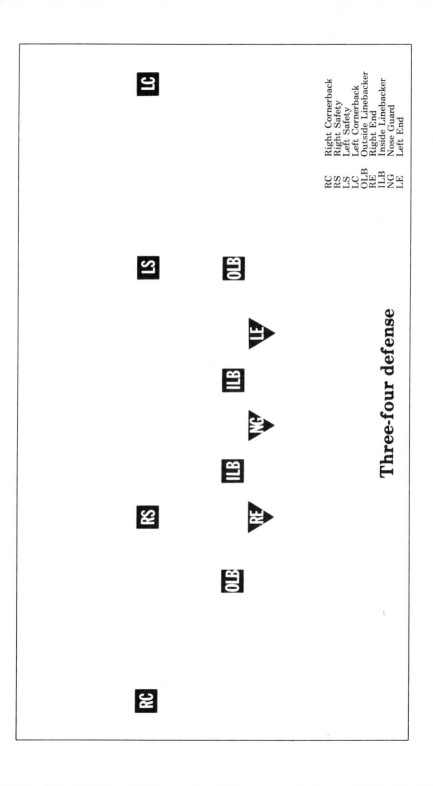

Three-four defense

RC   Right Cornerback
RS   Right Safety
LS   Left Safety
LC   Left Cornerback
OLB Outside Linebacker
RE   Right End
ILB Inside Linebacker
NG   Nose Guard
LE   Left End

Three-point stance. A pre-snap posture used by linemen, set backs, and flankers, in which only one hand is placed on the ground for balance.

Three-step punter. A kicker who uses an abnormal punting technique that allows him to gain more power but causes more risk of a blocked kick. Normal technique requires 1½ steps and less time.

Throw. To attempt a forward pass.

Throw it away. To attempt to throw an incomplete pass in an effort to avoid being sacked and losing yardage.

Throw under. To attempt short and medium range forward passes against the retreating defensive backs in a zone defense.

Tie. A game in which both teams have an equal number of points.

Tight end (TE). The strong-side end in the T-formation; the end on the line who is not split away from the tackle.

Timeout. A pause in the action requested by a team. It lasts 1½ minutes in intercollegiate play and 2 minutes in professional play. A team is allowed three charged timeouts in each half.

Timing up. A coordinated workout for the quarterback and his receivers, in which they practice the synchronization of all their pass plays.

Tipping the play. Revealing the direction of an offensive play by inadvertently showing a physical sign before the snap of the ball.

Title. Symbol of superiority over all other teams; ultimate goal of all teams. To possess the title means that the team has won the championship.

Title game. Matchup of the best two teams for the championship, which determines the No. 1 team in the league.

Toe. Nickname for the place kicker or team's best kicker.

Too much time. Violation of the allotted time for huddling and putting the ball in play. Penalty is five yards.

Toss. To throw the ball either forward or backward.

Touch football. A game of football in which there is no tackling, only tagging with the hands.

Touchback. A ball on or behind a team's goal line which is declared dead provided that the force which put the ball there came from the opposing team. The ball is put in play at the 20-yard line.

Touchdown (TD). Advancement of the ball through the plane of the opponent's goal line. The reward is six points and a try for a *conversion*.

Touchdown pass. A complete forward pass that advances the ball on or beyond the plane of the opponent's goal line.

Touchdown play. Any maneuver that physically advances the ball on or beyond the plane of the opponent's goal line.

Touchdown run. A rush across the plane of the opponent's goal line.

Tough yardage. Describes the area inside the opponent's 10-yard line, where the defense has less field to cover against a forward pass and can concentrate all of its manpower in defenses designed to stop rushing yardage.

Trade. An exchanging of one player or players to another club for one player or players.

Trailer pattern. A coordinated pass route taken by two receivers. They follow the same course downfield and break in opposite directions, trying to find a clear area after the defensive coverage commits itself.

Train. To work out; to condition the body for the demands of the game through exercise, practice, and proper diet.

Trainer. The overseer of a team's physical condition. He is in charge of physical preparation for games, such as taping the joints and the daily rehabilitation of injured players.

Training camp. A summer encampment at which new players try to make the team, veteran players condition themselves, and coaches apply fundamental training and teach playbook strategy.

Training room. An area close to the locker room where the trainer treats injured players and prepares them physically for practice and a game. Usually includes diathermy machines, weight training apparatus, and other medical equipment.

Training table. (1) A general term for the dietary conditioning of a team. (2) The place where the team eats special high-protein meals.

Trajectory. The path of a kickoff, punt, or forward pass.

Transfer of balance. To shift the weight and balance upon physical contact from one side of the body to the other. An intricate process perfected only by the most talented of ball carriers.

Trap. An offensive maneuver in which a defensive player is permitted to penetrate before he is blocked.

Trap block. A shoulder block or cross-body block by a pulling lineman or a set back on the side of a defensive player who has been allowed to penetrate the offensive backfield.

Traveling squad. The full roster of players who make trips to away games.

Trenches. Physical combat at the line of scrimmage between the offensive linemen and the defensive linemen.

Tri-captains. Three players chosen as captains either by a poll of the players or by the coaches.

Trick. Any coordinated action by defensive linemen other than orthodox straight-ahead penetration.

Trick play. Any offensive maneuver that includes a deceptive act, such as a reverse forward pass, multiple fakes, or a fake punt and pass.

Triple threat. A player who can run, pass, and kick.

Tripping. Using the feet or legs to knock down another player, including the ball carrier. The penalty is 15 yards.

Tuck. To place the football under the arm and hold it in the proper manner.

Turk. The mythical character who knocks at a player's door when he is cut from the squad. An imaginary training camp demon invoked by veterans who terrorize first-year players with taunts of "The Turk is coming!" as cutdown time draws near.

Turn the corner. To successfully sweep the end.

"Turn the play in." A defensive order for an outside player to contain the end sweep at all costs and make the ball carrier turn back inside toward the majority of defensive players.

Turn-in pattern. A pass route that takes a receiver straight downfield, driving the defensive coverage deep, before he stops sharply and trots a few steps back toward the inside.

Turning point. A play or event that reverses the trend of a game.

Turnover. A physical mistake, such as a fumble or an interception, that gives possession of the ball to the opponent.

TV timeout. A mandatory timeout called by the officials under orders from the television producer so that a commercial may be shown. Neither team is charged for it.

Twinkle toes. Nickname for a cute, agile, swift ball carrier who is not fond of physical contact.

Two-a-days. Practice sessions in both the morning and the afternoon during pre-season training.

Two-minute drill. A pre-planned ready list of offensive plays designed to save time and exploit the *prevent* defense. It is put into effect when time is running out in the half or at the end of a game.

Two-minute warning. Notification by the referee to both benches that two minutes remain in either the half or the game.

Two point conversion. An amateur football extra point option that gives the scoring team the choice of trying either a placement for one point or a rush or forward pass for two points from the three-yard line.

Two-way performer. A player who plays both offense and defense.

Umbrella defense. A variation of the 6-3-2 defense, which was the original anti–T-formation weapon. The emphasis is on pass defense. In the early days of the wide-open professional T-formation, it provided total pass coverage for the first time, because the defensive ends sprang outward toward the sidelines, instead of boxing or penetrating to stop the sweeps. This gave the defense an umbrellalike pass protection on the peripheral areas. The 6-1-4 defense assigned seven players with pass coverage responsibility rather than the normal five-player pass defense, which was common in the early 1950s. It was the acorn from which the modern 4-3-4 pro defense has grown.

Umpire (U). One of six officials who police the game. He is responsible mainly for legality of equipment, the coin toss, legality of blocks in the interior line, and the movements of linemen downfield on pass plays. Positioned behind the defensive line, he must be agile and quick to avoid injury because of his closeness to the combat of the linemen.

Unbalanced line. A formation that places more offensive linemen on one side of the center than on the other.

Undefeated. Refers to a team that has not lost any regular season game.

Underthrown. Refers to a pass that is delivered too weakly and falls incomplete in front of a receiver who is open. This weak delivery forces the pass receiver to stop and run back to make the completion.

Unhindered field goal try. A free kick executed from the site of a *fair catch*.

Uniform. A player's complete set of equipment: helmet, jersey, pants, shoulder pads, hip pads, stockings, and shoes.

Unity. Togetherness among players, coaches, and executives. Usually a sign of a competent hierarchy that knows how to select coaches who know how to judge talent and use it correctly.

Unnecessary roughness. Avoidable contact such as piling on, malicious contact out of bounds, or late tackling after the whistle. It is considered a personal foul, incurring a 15-yard penalty and possible ejection from the game.

Unsportsmanlike conduct. This type of violation includes oral abuse by players, coaches, executives or fans; emotional outcries or gestures on the part of same; and equipment infractions, such as tampering with the ball. Penalty: 15 yards and possible forfeit, if it continues unabated for an extended period of time.

Unsung. Underrated, unheralded; said of a player who does not get his just reward in honor among the fans or the media.

Up the middle. Describes any offensive activity directed toward the center of the field, such as a rush, pass, or kickoff return; a thrust into the center of the majority of defensive players.

Upback. The shallowest offensive back in the T-formation and the wishbone formation, generally the fullback.

Upended. Tackled, knocked down, turned upside-down by a low tackle.

Uprights. Two 20-foot standards that support the crossbar.

Upset. Unexpected victory by a team considered to be too weak for a superior opponent.

Use up the clock. To pass the time in the execution of repeated rushing plays in an effort to end the regulation game and protect a slim point lead.

Veer offense. An offensive system centering around a strong, fast quarterback who sprints to the tackle hole and either gives the ball to a running back or keeps it and runs around the end, if the linebacker has committed himself inside to stop a rush off-tackle. The quarterback also can pitch to the trailing back, as on the *option play*, if he isolates the linebacker outside, controlling the linebacker without even blocking him. A variation of the split T-formation and the *belly series*.

Veteran. A player or coach who has more than one year of experience.

Violation. An infraction of the rules governing the game. Also called a *foul*.

Visiting team. The team that travels to the game on the opponent's field or in its stadium.

Waggle. A play action passing strategy that is the opposite of the rollout, or nonpocket pass. The quarterback fakes a handoff and rolls away from the blocking and fake-rush flow with a minimum of blocking protection.

Waiver. The official procedure for releasing a player in professional football. An unwanted player is offered to every other club in the league, each of which may claim him in reverse order of the won-lost standings. If claimed by a club, the player may be retrieved from the waiver list, and his club may try to work out a trade in which something of value may be obtained. Otherwise, the club that claims the player is granted the rights to the player after a specified period of time and merely pays a minimal fee in return.

Waiver list. An official listing of players about to be released in professional football, which is circulated to every club via an electronic system.

Walkaway position. A revealing posture of an outside linebacker who has set up slightly deeper and looser than necessary prior to the snap of ball, tipping his mission: to help cover the short inside zone against the wide receiver lined up to his side.

Walkoff. Assessment of a penalty by an official.

Walk-on. An outstanding prospect who makes the team without the benefit of a scholarship in college football or without being drafted and signed to a professional contract. A prospect who makes the team unexpectedly without an official invitation.

Wall. A line of blockers that seals off a clear lane for the punt or kickoff return man.

Ward off. To repulse an attack; to fight off a block by stiff-arming a tackler.

Water boy. A volunteer who carries the water bucket or tank out to the players on the field.

Water bucket. The vessel used for storage of drinking water, which is transported to the players during official pauses in the game.

Waterbug. Slang for a very fast player who can change direction instantly and unpredictably.

Weak safety. See *Free safety*.

Weak side. The side of the offense opposite the tight end (strong-side end) and the flanker (wide receiver) in T-formation and I-formation alignments; the side that sets up with the least amount of linemen on its side of the center in any unbalanced line formation.

Wedge. A four-player blocking line that retreats after the kickoff and leads the kickoff return man in a pre-determined direction. Four blockers generally line up 20 yards in front of the kickoff return men.

Wedge-breaker. A daring member of the kickoff unit, who must charge into the four-man kickoff return wedge and try to occupy as many of the blockers as possible so that other members of his unit can reach the kickoff return man.

Weight room. An exercise area beneath the stadium stands or in the club office building that contains weightlifting apparatus and isometric equipment used for players' body-building programs.

Weight training. Off-season and seasonal body-building programs using weightlifting apparatus and isometric exercises.

Wheels. Slang for a player's legs.

Whirlpool treatment. Diathermic soothing of an injury; a system of warm water massage that promotes healing.

Wide open. Description of an offensive player who is not covered by a defensive player.

Wide-open game. All-out offensive attempts by both teams despite field position and tendency charts. Predominance of passing attempts for both teams.

Wide receiver (WR). (1) The split or weak-side end who lines up on the opposite side of a tight end. (2) The flanker back who lines up three to six yards outside the tight end.

Wild card. A playoff berth in professional football, filled by the second-place team with the best won-lost record in each of the National Football League's two conferences. The qualifying teams join the three divisional champions in each conference in the semifinal round of the championship playoffs each season.

Will. Play-book term for the weak-side linebacker on defense.

Wind sprints. A series of graduated running drills designed to build stamina and leg strength. Used during training camp and before and after seasonal practices.

Winding down. Adjustment of emotional level that takes place in the locker room after a game.

Wing. Media jargon for throwing arm.

Wingback. The offensive backfield position located behind or slightly outside either end.

Winner. A player whose heroic capabilities frequently emerge in crucial situations.

Winning record. The statistics of a team that has more victories than losses.

Wishbone formation. An offensive alignment similar to the full house T-formation except that the fullback (upback) lines up a yard in front of the halfbacks instead of a yard deeper than the halfbacks. Created by the University of Texas' Darrell Royal, the alignment is primarily a rushing system, generating added inside blocking strength from the strategic location of the upback, who can lead either halfback into the interior holes as well as quickly combine with one of the halfbacks to lead the other halfback in awesome ground thrusts. The tight alignment also provides the quarterback with the devastating triple-option potential. This aspect exploits the tightness of the defensive linebackers, who must sit longer for fakes to the backs in the interior holes and lose valuable time in pursuit of the quarterback when he keeps the ball and runs around the end or pitches to a sweeping halfback.

Wound up. At a high emotional pitch; results in fanatical player conduct on the field.

Wrist action. An integral part of the passing technique; the flexing of the wrist in the passing motion.

X. (1) Symbol for a defensive player in strategy diagrams. (2) A term describing a crossing action among running backs, pass receivers, offensive blockers (X-block), and defensive players. (3) Play-book nomenclature for the weak-side wide receiver. (4) A defensive stunt in which the two tackles cross in an attempt to confuse the blockers and sack the forward passer.

X block. See under *X*.

Y. Play-book nomenclature for the strong-side (tight) end.

Yard. A three-foot section of the field.

Yard line. The specific position of the ball in relation to the goal line.

Yard marker. A sign on the sideline that identifies the yard line.

Yardage. Accumulation or loss of yards.

Z. Play-book nomenclature for the strong-side wide receiver or flanker.

Zigout. A short pass route for wide receivers, which takes them on Z-shaped pattern.

Zigzag. Cutting back and forth; the movement of a rusher taking a crooked course through the defensive team.

Zing. Media expression meaning to criticize someone.

Zip. Description of the velocity of a bullet forward pass; a pass taking a powerfully fast course.

Zipper. Player slang for a scar.

Zone. (1) A portion of the field. (2) Division of offensive or defensive responsibility according to segments of field area.

Zone block. An offensive blocking assignment that is determined by area responsibility instead of by man or position responsibility.

Zone coverage. Overall distribution of pass defense assignments according to a specific area instead of a specific player.

Referee Hand Signals

Timeout

Touchdown, field goal

Personal foul

Illegal use of hands

Illegal contact

Illegal motion

First down

Delay of game

Holding

Offside or encroaching

Incomplete pass, penalty refused, missed kick

Pass interference